# Children Learning
# to Read

A Good Book Fascinates

# Children Learning to Read

## A Guide for Parents and Teachers

SEYMOUR W. ITZKOFF

PRAEGER

Westport, Connecticut
London

**Library of Congress Cataloging-in-Publication Data**

Itzkoff, Seymour W.
    Children learning to read : a guide for parents and teachers /
Seymour W. Itzkoff.
       p.  cm.
    Includes bibliographical references (p.  ) and index.
    ISBN 0-275-95436-6 (alk. paper)
    1. Reading.  2. Reading readiness.  I. Title.
LB1050.I885  1996
372.4—dc20      95-37653

British Library Cataloguing in Publication Data is available.

Library of Congress Catalog Card Number: 95-37653
ISBN: 0-275-95436-6

First published in 1996

Praeger Publishers, 88 Post Road West, Westport, CT 06881
An imprint of Greenwood Publishing Group, Inc.

Printed in the United States of America

The paper used in this book complies with the
Permanent Paper Standard issued by the National
Information Standards Organization (Z39.48-1984).

10 9 8 7 6 5 4 3 2

**Copyright Acknowledgments**

Excerpt from *Case Studies in Whole Language* by Richard T. Vacca and
Timothy V. Rasinski, copyright © 1992 by Holt, Rinehart and Winston,
Inc. Reprinted by permission of the publisher.

Every reasonable effort has been made to trace the owners of copyright
materials in this book, but in some instances this has proven impossible.
The author and publisher will be glad to receive information leading to
more complete acknowledgments in subsequent printings of the book
and in the meantime extend their apologies for any omissions.

To
*Julie and Heidi*
*for*
*Nathaniel and Lucy Rose*

# Contents

# Illustrations

**FIGURES**

## TABLES

# *Acknowledgments*

Much of the inspiration for the writing of this book has come from yearly interactions with my Smith College students in the course that I teach, "The Reading Process." My earlier book on reading, *How We Learn to Read* (1986), was also a product of the study of the reading process that I undertook with my students since I started to teach this course in 1972.

Much earlier and simultaneous experiences—teaching in the public schools, supervision, the Directorship for a number of years of the Smith College Campus School—all added to the grist of knowledge from psycholinguistic theory that supported the argument of the earlier book as well as the present effort.

*How We Learn to Read*, being more directed to the questions that students of education asked of the situation in reading instruction, opened the door to the issues that are raised in this volume. Simply, students, teachers, and parents all kept raising and asking questions. And I kept on reading, thinking, and browsing around classrooms and wise teachers of reading.

Marianne Schumann of the Willie Ross School for the Deaf, in Longmeadow, Massachusetts, an institution on whose board I have proudly served, revealed many of the mysteries of language learning and reading that these brave youngsters must experience and master. Dr. Donna Park of the Northampton, Massachusetts Public Schools opened the door to Reading Recovery, a challenging and necessary addition to the elementary reading program that is now sweeping the United States.

My colleagues in the Smith College Campus School have, in their recent commitment to whole language reading and invented spelling, forced me to analyze quite carefully the special circumstances under which such teaching in reading can be successful, as well as the more perilous outcomes of its wider, less exclusive application to more typical American school settings.

The editing and general editorial guidance that Patricia Stroman once more provided to me in the development of the argument of the book cannot be overestimated. As always, I must underline her indispensability in the completion of this project.

Of special note in the research and bibliographical development of this book has been the contribution of my research assistant, Ruth Ann Polk. Her knowledge of the literature in reading and her understanding of the reading process have allowed me to shape the ideas expressed in this book into a much more coherent argument. She stayed with the project until we could see it through. And for that I am deeply appreciative.

The research and study of this mysterious ability of humans, to read and to write, is not yet over. I hope that I will continue to encounter curious people—teachers, parents, and students—who will ask difficult and intriguing questions.

# Introduction

Once upon a time, reading didn't matter that much. To a family of good intelligence living on the frontier, the challenges of raw nature were complex enough. Even in recent generations, a farmer, wood-cutter, auto mechanic, or neighborhood fixer-upper might get along without being able to read, or need to read only at a rudimentary level, enough to sign his or her name or decipher basic road, street, or other signs. Those days are gone forever. A new world beckons—has beckoned for several decades.

In the old days, teachers were taught in their professional courses to be sensitive to their students' emotional and confidence levels. Parent-child relationships were scrutinized for any signs that the tensions that could often be observed in dysfunctional families were having any impact on the learning abilities of the child.

Reading problems were viewed as sure signs that all was not right with the emotional health of the child. However, more study, observation, and sophistication in understanding the nature of learning, and, in particular, reading, began to reveal something new.

This was the realization that the relationship was probably reversed. Many children from dysfunctional families, children with real emotional and personality handicaps, were doing fine in reading. On the other hand, many children from apparently functional, economically successful families, "well put-together" kids, were failing in reading. Often the emotional disabilities appeared to be direct consequences of this failure. There is nothing worse for the confidence and educational well-being of children than failure to progress in the reading skills on a level equal with their peers.

Reading and the skills—computer and others—that flow from reading's basic intellectual operations today dominate a world that ever more rapidly is distancing itself from primary or direct contact with nature. We live in a universe that is increasingly symbolic, from computer languages, math and statistical techniques, and musical notation, to the entire process of confronting the modern abstract technostructure of our world society.

Reading is basic because it essentially is the subbasement of this structure of knowledge. New upper stories are continuously being added in ever new complexity. But the basic skills of thinking that are opened up in the first primer featuring Dick, Jane, and Spot, elaborated in almost infinite variety, rest on a basic set of primary intellective processes which must be developed if one is to call oneself educated.

In fact, it is fair to say that all those dozens of reading, vocabulary, and paragraph understanding tests that we took during our school years reflect a grim reality that we must now come to grips with. Indeed, other forms of human intelligence are tapped by modern vocational challenges. But it is also probably correct that a reading test, except in the case of a clinically diagnosed reading-disabled dyslexic, measures the long-term intellectual possibilities of an individual better than any other test of a person's skills.

This is because through reading and literacy flows a human being's perception of experience and knowledge. All other tests usually give us narrower pictures of a person's specific skills and knowledge. (One word that we can use for these latter potencies is *talent*.) Reading skills and the understanding or comprehension that flows from them seem in some mysterious way to predict an individual's general and long-range potential for learning and growth.

That is why it is so important that we, as parents and educators, give the literacy requirements of children's schooling experience the utmost in effort and understanding. We must clear away the mythologies, the ideological propaganda, even the "educationese" jargon that the profession often uses to keep inquiring parents at bay.

In this book, we are going to start at the beginning. Indeed, it *is* important to understand how children learn to read. Too many children, and often adolescents and adults, too, have been crippled in their ability to read rapidly and pleasurably, then with concentration and efficiency, because of the misguided pseudo-theories that teachers have forced upon parents and then their children. Often, unknowing teachers are seduced into thinking that a highly touted new method is the latest breakthrough in knowledge, when in reality it is the imposition of just one more form of educational zealotry posing as truth.

Starting in the 1920s, the struggle was the classical one over the so-called sight approach to reading, which was then being argued for by educators awed by the experimental results from use of the tachistoscope, invented in the 1880s. As will be discussed later, the tachistoscope projected images of words and letters on a screen for very brief moments of time. Surprisingly, individuals were able to identify the images—in this case, five words—as easily as they could identify five letters.

Yet the general curricular program of look-say, that is, the sight approach that grew from this knowledge, was never able to explain why many children failed to learn to read well through the use of this method. In the 1950s, the old-line phonics people finally succeeded in relegating look-say to the outfield. Sad to say, they, in turn, created millions of readers who, essentially, were crippled.

Children taught exclusively through the various versions of systematic phonics programs (rules to be memorized *ad infinitum*), might be able to decode a word to its sound equivalent, but their reading speeds were so slow and halting that often by the time they got to the end of a sentence they had forgotten the beginning. Reading as a result of teaching through the phonics approach was often painful and frustrating. Essentially, systematic phonics instruction in the many thousands of classrooms where it was imposed created a generation of individuals who would not pick up a book. Many such readers were defeated in their life ambitions and potential before they ever started. They never had an educational chance.

Still, some phonics instruction is important. I will try to show why, how, and where.

The battles still go on. In the old days, because the educational profession supported the sight approach, using whole-word recognition as the key to reading instruction, and because the leadership cadres in the profession were usually liberals of the Norman Thomas/Socialist variety, or possibly Franklin Roosevelt–style liberal Democrats, look-say was deemed a radical political conspiracy by many of the political right. Naturally, the phonics people, especially in their advocacy by the Council for Basic Education, an old-line, right-wing organization, became the bastion for the eventual liberal defeat in the 1950s. And with it came the infatuation with reading viewed as decoding, or phonics.

Now the warriors are at it again. This time, the phonics people are lining up against the whole-language advocates, again a large assemblage of professional educators, including many teachers. While not politically or ideologically tinged, as in the earlier reading wars, this new uproar echoes with clear signs of a new educational disarray, 1980–1990s style. In a time of declining educational achievement levels, such battles are to be expected. The public begins a desperate search for reasons for the current literacy disaster.

Certainly, the question of reading must be the centerpiece of any educational debate. This is especially urgent, as we have recently— in 1993—been presented with some staggeringly fearful literacy statistics in a study sponsored by the Department of Education in Washington, D.C. Fully 50 percent of our American youngsters who have been in our schools at least eight years, at the end of their high school education are essentially illiterate when it comes to world-class economic functionality.

There is absolutely no reason for our concern to be translated into another ideological debate over methodology. The knowledge as to how children learn to read is in the public domain. It is there for all to share. It is my intention that the analysis to be presented in the following pages will dispel some of the myths of misinformation, even the artificial controversies that are now tearing apart what should be a joint and cooperative effort by teachers and families.

Having two warring camps of reading instruction is a waste. The different methods, now at opposite poles, are in truth two natural stages in the reading process through which the vast majority of children pass on their way to fluency, comprehension, and pleasure. I will explain this. Please read on.

# Chapter 1

# *Baby Speaks*

## THE NATURAL LANGUAGE: SPEECH

Language makes the difference for your child. Otherwise a child would be only a bit more than a smart chimpanzee. Some think that language, even in its rudimentary beginnings many millions of years ago, when humans were relatively small of brain, led to the brain's expansion and pushed our intelligence over the "Rubicon" to humanity.

Every child born of a human mother and father, brought up in a social environment where people speak the native language within the hearing of the child, will learn to speak. To an observer, the gradual blossoming of language in the child after twelve months of age seems miraculous.

The child goes from one-word statements such as "Da-Da," "milky," "bye-bye"—to short sentences such as "I go out" and "I sit down"—and from funny words to command words. Gradually the sphere of meaning—of communication—emerges, and the child enters our world, a society of both freedom and restraint.

**Table 1.1**
**Timeline of Reading and Writing Development**

*Birth to One Year Old*
Lalling, babbling, cooing (and crying) are major forms of communication.

*One Year Old*
One-word sentences are spoken—"cookie."

*Two Years Old*
Short, two- and three-word sentences are beginning to be formed—"Me want cookie."

*Three Years Old*
Early Readers
Virtuoso, early fluent readers begin to emerge.
Fluent decoders identified—children who, early on, can decode words into their sound equivalents.
Children can pick out and remember distinct sounds—being able to distinguish the short "a" sound in "cat."

*Four Years Old*
Remember shapes of letters. For example, children can often learn to write their names without being able to identify the actual letters in their names.
Development of sound recognition abilities.

*Five Years Old*
Knowledge of letter names emerges.
Telling of and listening to stories.
Shape recognition.
Associating words with pictures.

*Six Years Old*
Mediated Reading
Child decodes words into sound equivalents before attaining the meaning.
Matching of sounds with letters.
Spelling in writing approximates conventional spelling.
Understanding of sound differences without rules. For example, knowing automatically that the "e" in "meet" is pronounced as a long "e."
Early Fluent Reading
Less reliance on decoding to sound. Decoding used when necessary, but more often reading directly for meaning.
Reading Recovery intervention necessary if trouble moving into or through mediated and early fluent reading.

**Table 1.1** (continued)

---

Seven Years Old
 Fluent Reading
  Children move past decoding into reading directly for meaning.
  Spelling moves closer to, if not already into standard spelling.
  Diagnosis for specific reading and other learning disabilities should be made
   now, not later, to prevent exacerbation of learning difficulties.

*Eight Years Old*
 Children should be well into rapid fluent reading for meaning.
 Children are reading on their own both for enjoyment and to gain information
  in the various subject matters.

---

Language gives tangibility to the brain's desire to know and control. It gives concrete possibility to the child's urge to enter into voluntary friendships, to play or not to play, to like someone or something, or not, and to behave in ways that a human without language could never hope to behave.

Think of a child born profoundly deaf, with an intelligence that is keen and perceptive, a child full of dynamic energies. But she cannot hear the natural language, the words, sentences, the subtleties of nuance in speech. Without powerful educational intervention to create the semblance of speech equivalents, is it not true that nature has shorn from this human at least half her perceptual intelligence, her possibilities to master her world?

She cannot communicate to the stranger who does not sign. Even if she is taught to speak—for her vocal chords and other speech structures are intact—she will need special and laborious instruction to learn to articulate speech as well as to read and write. Without such help, she might never enter that larger language world that could empower her intelligence to reach out to dreams of knowledge and understanding that speech alone could open for her. Indeed, teachers of the deaf refer to the development of literacy for hearing-impaired youngsters as teaching such children the visual form of their natural language.

Literacy is, of course, dependent and built upon the foundation gained by children through their natural language and the culture from which this language arises. The following story may help us to understand how important culture is for the child when she first hears language.

## CULTURE AND LANGUAGE

These events took place in the early 1960s. An American university professor and his wife, without children, wished to adopt. They decided after some investigation to adopt an infant that had been placed in an orphanage in Korea shortly after her birth. By the time the child arrived in the United States, she was about six months old.

This was a child well-loved in her new home. The parents tried to do everything right. They spent much time speaking and playing with the child. However, by the time the child was beginning to speak full, if simple, sentences, at the age of about a year and a half, the parents began to suspect that their assumed understanding and knowledge of the relationship between language and nurture were wrong.

The child spoke in English with a decided Korean accent, despite all the enriched environmental American stimulation, including neighborhood playmates, that they had provided. Why? It could not be genes, they assured themselves. Everyone *knew* that there were no specific genes that could determine that a child would speak with the sounds, accents, and phonemes of her native Korean ethnicity!

The family discussed the situation with a colleague from the department of linguistics. He asked how long the child had been in the Korean orphanage. "Almost six months" was the reply. "Well," said the linguist, "you must understand that even though the infant could only gurgle and coo, in terms of her developmental speech patterns, regardless of where she was born, she still listened and heard the sounds around her."

In short, the child was listening *in Korean*, and thus spontaneously and automatically reinforcing even in her beginning sounds the patterns she had heard early on. In the process, many other sound possibilities that she could have expressed in other languages were suppressed, including the sounds that later could be formed into the English language.

Naturally this child, as she learned to speak and express increasingly complex ideas, and in interaction with her new American environment, more and more imitated the sound structure of the actual language she was learning. Eventually she spoke beautifully enunciated and grammatically correct English.

But she taught us all an important lesson. It is that the intelligence and the sensitivity of the child to the world around her, as well as to her own demanding biological and personal needs, are mobilized at an early stage in her development. Many parents can remember how their not-yet-one-year-old child would react to such expressions as "Suzy, look who has come to see you . . . Grandpa!" or "Where is the clock on the dresser, Bobby?" or "Would you like to go outside?"

Try it out for yourself. Very young children's responses to these and many other kinds of statements and questions will persuade you that children learn early to understand both that the purpose of language is to communicate, and the meaning of words and sentences. It is often not merely an intelligent guess on their part; babies seem to truly understand what people around them are saying.

## PRINCIPLES

Here are two interesting dimensions to the natural language learning of very young children, principles that we can use when we turn to the problem of how a child learns to read.

1. Long before she is able to articulate word meanings and the sounds (phonemes) that make up words, as well as the grammar of a sentence, the infant is already listening to the sounds of the language spoken around her. The process of listening is not passive. It is active and probably different in every child. The result of this listening process is that the child will start spontaneously to construct a lexicon of the sounds she has heard. These will constitute building blocks of her natural spoken language.

From time immemorial, literally millions of spoken languages have been created by humans. We humans are able to create a vast variety of sounds—consonants, vowels, clicks, grunts—all because we have a remarkably flexible vocal apparatus. Our potential for creating different sound structures for the various human spoken languages contrasts vividly with the limited set of stereotyped screeches that any primate species can utter.

At the same time that the infant is listening and creating this lexicon of sounds that will become her own personal repertoire of speech sounds several months down the line, she is repressing, often permanently, all those millions of sound possibilities (phones) that infants in other linguistic cultures need for later use.

At the same time, since most children are extremely plastic in their language and speech learning skills in the early years, they can often quickly learn a new language if transported into a new culture. This is why elementary-school-age youngsters are able to learn a foreign language so much more easily than adults.

2. At the same time that a child is being immersed in the spoken language of the family and culture around her, her automatic language understanding system is activated. All this occurs long before her speech system matures. The child first internalizes the sounds of the natural and native language around her. Then, she begins to understand language in a general way, as it is used by adult family members, often beginning with the understanding of simple words, questions, and statements. The child understands what she hears before she can express these language elements vocally.

This is not to say that the child does not want to respond in kind—to say something. However, the child's developmental processes for speech expression are slower to mature than the more passive hearing and understanding structures that are necessary for achieving these same basic concepts.

Later we will explain how this very similar *independently variable* set of factors goes into making each child a unique example of the learning-to-read process. This means that just as each child's language listening and speech skills develop to a different rhythm and sequence, so, too, in the reading process there are independently variable elements in a child's learning profile. They develop and mature at different times and with differing emphases for each youngster. These have to be respected when the school's instructional program is begun.

## ALL CHILDREN ARE DIFFERENT

All parents would naturally be overjoyed to see their children progress smoothly in learning to read, and then progress into fluent reading for comprehension as well as pleasure. One of the elements in the success or failure of any child in learning any subject matter is the naturalness of the learning process, the sense of flow and mastery.

Success often depends on the cues that children receive from the authority figures around them, from their teachers or parents.

Adult concern cannot be hidden from the youngster. Children have always been able to see through the ruses that teachers use to disguise groupings in reading and other curriculum areas. They quickly catch on to the idea that the "tulips" are the dopes and the "daisies" are the geniuses.

The point in all of this is that children, from birth to the middle years of childhood, eight to eleven, have such wildly deviating developmental rates that the so-called rules of development, especially in the language areas, ought to be tossed out. This is especially true if your child is named George or Al, in short, a male, so often "learning vulnerable," and often "behind the girls." This is true in the language-developing years, both in speech acquisition and later, in the process of learning to read. By the end of the middle years, ten or eleven years of age, boys have usually caught up with their female classmates.

This variability is understandable from the standpoint of human development, especially in the language acquisition area. It will be even more understandable in the area of reading. Our language ability has been explained by scientists as being the only specialization in humans that radically departs from the patterns of our simian ancestors. Certainly, we are brainier. But this is a quantitative increase. Nothing like the various language areas in the human brain, in addition to its two distinctly functioning hemispheres, is to be found in the apes.

Because of the many differently developing language functions in the child, wired as they are to other parts of the brain, as well as to the more basic neurological structure of the central nervous system, there will always be striking differences in children's development. There will also be strikingly differing strengths and weaknesses in their language skills—their listening, speaking, understanding, and articulating.

Accept such differences in the basic acquisition of the natural language, and expect such differences either to be reproduced or transformed (you cannot predict which) as your child begins to transfer the skills of the spoken language (language by ear) to the written form (language by sight). Differences between children from birth to eight years of age in this regard are often enough to scare any conscientious, loving parent. Why isn't she like mom or dad, or like older brother Jim? Hold it! Such differences don't necessarily bear on the ultimate development or fruition of your child's intellectual power.

Some children speak early, learn late. Some are precocious, others are late bloomers in everything. Naturally, better early, most parents will exclaim. But then comes the plateau. You simply cannot predict. Just be aware that intelligence itself changes in its development. The ten-year-old wizard becomes the sixteen-year-old just one of the bunch, and vice versa.

An interesting set of experiments reported in the scientific literature of the last several years shows the limits of parental or family influence on the development of the spoken language in very young children. Simply, there does not seem to be any relationship between the promptings of vocabulary or sentence structure that parents communicate to young children twelve to twenty-four months old and the form and substance of the "baby talk" that the little ones use to find their way into the linguistic family of humans.

These babies certainly hear the language of their parents and older siblings. These external inputs are crucial for their ability to internalize human language as they hear and experience it. But the output, how this linguistic experience is mobilized to stimulate the child to begin speaking, issues forth from the inner recesses of the young child's evolving individuality. It comes out pure Suzy or Jimmy, and each child within the family will be different. Try it out for yourself, and delight in your child's uniqueness.

For a bit of linguistic insurance, as much as you can, keep your infant around adults as well as children. Don't isolate or protect her from the noisy world outside. She will sleep, often amidst relative cacophony. Importantly, when children are awake and maturing, they will be listening to people speaking and behaving, thus being inaugurated into the human world of language, its causes and effects. And above all, don't speak baby talk to your child! They will respond in kind.

## SUMMARY

The mystery and opportunity lies in the inner individuality of the child. It is important to understand as we prepare the ground for a child's encounter with the written word that it is an inner self that must absorb these external marks and scribbles. Much will depend on the evolving depth of individual understanding that lies within each unique child.

As we will point out in some detail later, parents and teachers can do only so much to help a child learn to read. It has to come from the inside out. We can set up the external environment in a way that we hope will trigger the child's developmental readiness. And the child *should* begin to read.

Thus, this message about the process of acquiring the natural spoken language will illuminate the reading process. Speech comes from within the child. It is a process of taking the sounds of the external world and applying them to that inner semantic kernel of meaning that the child is driven to express.

It will begin with one-word sentences, clearly expressed in the home language—English, French, Chinese, or whatever. Then, almost miraculously, comes a sense of grammatical appropriateness—nouns, verbs, prepositions, clauses, and sentences—real structures of articulated meaning. None of these will be externally determined by a parent or teacher. Rather, the child assimilates the outside stimuli, the talking, conversation, family squabbles and all, and bends and shapes this linguistic matter like putty into the developmental specialness of her own individuality.

It is a universal process. It is happening to all children throughout the world, our humanity expressed in the uniqueness of our native culture's language. Finally, it is digested, absorbed, and expressed personally as part of the natural variability of each individual child.

It is a biological miracle, created because of as-yet-unknown processes and evolutionary shapings over a period of many millions of years in the evolution of *Homo sapiens sapiens*. It is from these natural gifts—language and intelligence—that that once-rare skill, literacy, now the essential denominator of educational competence and social success, will be crafted.

# Chapter 2

# *Our Alphabet: Language by Ear and by Eye*

**FROM SPEAKING TO READING**

Your child is three or four years old. She speaks, she plays, she loves to be loved. She is a delight. Soon the preschool beckons. In such programs, play and socialization reign. The children get to know and interact with other children of their own age. In the most subtle ways, they obtain all sorts of skills that they will need in order to live together with others in a dynamic, complex world, a world created by their peers.

To be a mistress of this world and not its servant, she will need to know how to read. It is the key to thinking, then to writing and even creating. "There's power in those words"—words by eye, which ultimately have been derived from words by ear.

We want to give this child every advantage ahead of time to enable her to master the complexities and the abstractness of the written word. Because she is only three or four years old, we do not know, and cannot predict, how she will master the skill of reading. She may talk a mile a minute, she may inundate us with her blab. Yet other things are necessary besides her speaking/language skills, even aside from her delighting "brightness," her evident intelligence.

If we are concerned parents and wish to spend our time with our children well, we will consider the problem of transition, from a speaking child to a reading one. What is involved?

## SOUNDS AND MEANING

We need to understand the nature of the reading challenge to the average American, or, indeed, European child, for our languages are related, especially to the extent that they are languages built around the alphabetic principle. This means that, to a lesser or greater extent, these languages attempt to mirror the main sounds of the spoken language in the symbols of the written language.

To be sure, our own language is a hodge-podge. We have twenty-six letters, which in their various combinations represent the forty-four basic sounds of our language that we recognize as being distinct. These "public sounds"—we call them *phonemes*—represent CBS/Newscaster English. Not the drawl of the Texan, not the twang of the New Englander, not the Carolinian's purr. It is hard to say how many different phonemes a child would have to learn if we tried to mimic all these sounds in our written system.

This is one of the mysteries of reading, and the relationship of language by ear and by eye. For, as the once advocates of a separate reading system for African-American children—Black English—and the national scientific community, too, have learned, it really doesn't matter to the reader what the traditional alphabet looks like. This is because whether the language is spoken with a Texas drawl or a Maine twang, every child or adult automatically translates the letters and words that they see into their own spoken phonemic version of what they read.

As long as, when the child or adult reads a book or newspaper out loud in her home American accent, she is not corrected and told that she is wrong (which she is not), no harm is done. This is because, what people are really doing when they read is translating the marks on the paper *not into sounds, but into meaning*. The accent may or may not get in the way.

For example, let us say a person has heard a difficult word pronounced in CBS English on television. A day later, she happens to read it out loud from a newspaper in her own accent, even sounding it out for herself. She might or might not realize that it is the same word that she had heard the day before.

A difficult word such as "contemplate" or "persuasive" read or spoken in a different context and with a somewhat different meaning, since they earlier sounded so different also, might not ring the bell of relatedness. Think of all the vernacular pronunciations possible of certain common words. Compare them, for instance, when you are watching a British Television comedy. It might help you to understand why one roughly orthodox spoken version of the language would be preferable, though it is not required.

We can understand individuals from all over the United States with all their different accents. The reason is that our minds search beyond the sounds of the words or sentences, to go to the meanings that are being expressed. The truth, then, is that no separate spelling or orthographic system is necessary for the many different regional American accents or dialects, despite their different pronunciations of the common language, to enable all Americans to read more easily. Teachers and parents must disregard "odd" pronunciations by the child, as long as they do not disturb the child when she is learning to read.

The key question must be: Is the child understanding what she is reading? Is she transforming the letter sounds, words, and sentences into a meaningful story even when her spoken accent may not mirror what educational orthodoxy deems the proper pronunciation for reading orally?

## WRITING, READING, AND POWER

It may come as a surprise to many of us that the alphabetic system is not the only orthographic key to literacy. In the history of writing and reading, the Sumerians, ancient residents of the Middle East Tigris and Euphrates river basin, now modern Iraq, in *circa* 3500 B.C. evolved a written language system. The system was first based on picture meanings. The Egyptians took up this discovery and fully developed it into its system of hieroglyphics.

Soon, however, it was found that pictures were too vague, and often cumbersome. The pictures for homonyms, such as "sun" and "son," were often confusing and needed modification by a separate written mark, and plurals also required a special notation. Gradually, these modifications necessitated and helped to evolve these picture symbols into ever more abstract marks of meaning.

The Sumerians and then their successors, the Babylonians, gradually evolved a system of consonant syllables, usually with the vowels only implied and not written down. Hebrew, especially in its classical Semitic form, is an example of such a system widespread in the Middle East in that biblical era.

It took the ancient Greeks, skillful adapters of the best ideas around the Mediterranean Sea, to take the names of the Semitic consonants and vowels, from the Semitic Phoenician (today Phoenicia is Lebanon) sea peoples and adapt them to their own, very different spoken language. Thus, "aleph" became "alpha," "beth" became "beta," and "gimel" became "gamma." The result was the unique development of a fully alphabetic language with one letter (grapheme) for each of the sounds of their spoken language.

Why did they do this? At first, the usual function of literacy in the Middle East was to gain privilege and power. Literacy placed the great religious and mythological traditions of these societies at the beck and call of the priests. Only the priests could read the "truths of the gods," and thus they could guide the ordinary uneducated peasantry. Literacy also empowered the aristocracy and business community. It became an invaluable skill for handling large amounts of information, contracts, surveys, records, and provision lists. Such skills were handed down from father to son, as in the medieval guild system. They provided opportunities for wealth and power. The impact of literacy has not changed to this day.

It was the alphabetic principle, however, that made the democratic dissemination of power possible. Alphabetic writing, linked as it was to the sounds of the spoken language, was a relatively simple code for the average Greek or Roman citizen to break and understand. They tell the story of Athenian peasants coming into the great city for the festivals. Part of the celebrations were devoted either to literary and dramatic competitions, or to the replaying of some of the classical winners from previous festivals. These country people—"dustyfeet" was their colloquial description—would arrive in the predawn darkness, sitting outside the gates of the theater, munching on the contents of their goatskin bags, a breakfast of garlic and onions. At the break of daylight, they could be found reading rental copies of the play that was to be presented that morning. Such was the literary interest and command of the Athenian peasants.

**Table 2.1**
**Development of the Alphabet**

| ENGLISH | EGYPTIAN HIEROGLYPH | ABU-SIMBEL | MOABITE STONE | IONIAN GREEK |
|---|---|---|---|---|
| A | | | | |
| B | | | | |
| G | | | | |
| D | | | | |
| E | | | | |
| F(W) | | | | |
| Z | | | | |
| H | | | | |
| TH | | | | |
| I | | | | |
| K | | | | |
| L | | | | |
| M | | | | |
| N | | | | |
| X(SH) | | | | |
| O | | | | |
| P | | | | |
| S | | | | |
| Q | | | | |
| R | | | | |
| S | | | | |
| T | | | | |
| Ü | | | | |
| P-H | | | | |
| KH | | | | |
| PS | | | | |
| Ô | | | | |

The Romans created the spacing between words and systematized the writing of speeches, declarations, and documents so that they consistently went from left to right, and not curved around, left-right, right-left, as was sometimes the case with the Greeks. The Romans brought the alphabetic principle to its modern form. They also created state educational systems that attempted to bring all children from the age of seven on, both boys and girls, under the sway of Roman literate culture. Of course, the schooling was not always public, especially in the early years. Here, the streets of Rome resounded to the lash of birches and phonic choruses, as the pedagogues—more like drill masters—attempted to civilize the children of the rough-and-ready cities.

One more contrasting system of reading and writing should be mentioned, the Chinese. Of all the great civilizations, the Chinese acquired literacy last, between 2000 and 1500 B.C. Most authorities believe that the concept of writing was brought from the west by members of the Shang Dynasty, apparently a Persian type of people who used a form of picture writing.

The isolation of China during subsequent centuries caused the evolution of the Chinese system of literacy to develop in a highly distinctive manner. The elitist and central organization of the various dynastic regimes in China put a premium on making literacy a specialized, private skill, closely controlled by the state authorities. Thus was initiated the complex and difficult examination system of the Imperial Civil Service.

The result was that the Mandarin Chinese writing system evolved without recourse to the sound system of the spoken language. The system of symbols, characters, ideographs, logographs, or whatever one calls them, represents words and phrases, not as sound replications, but more as ideas.

To read Chinese, or, indeed, any one of the other Chinese-derivative writing systems (such as the Japanese *Kanji*) requires the learning and memorization of literally thousands of characters before one can read even basic meaningful written material. It is quite different from the simple Dick, Jane, and Spot that our children can learn to read with simple constructions based on the sound system of spoken English.

The result is that our children get a much quicker start toward literacy. But, because our written system is so irregular, one can't count on words to be spelled alike just because they sound alike, such as "tale" and "tail." And even if words are spelled similarly,

**Figure 2.1**
**Chinese Writing Not Dependent on Sound Equivalents**

they may sound very different, as in "enough" and "though." This is one reason why the teaching of reading raises so much dust and confusion. English is a phonetically irregular alphabetic language.

Still, we must admire the young readers of Mandarin Chinese. They cannot fall back on their knowledge of the spoken language for assistance with a knotty phrase. It turns out that because the written language evolved as an elite skill for a small, guild-like group of educated rulers, who spoke privately to each other in their monkish cloisters, either in Xi'an, the early capital, or in Beijing, the traditional ruling center, the spoken versions of Mandarin Chinese became mutually unintelligible in different parts of China. The spoken language drifted apart, as it always does when groups of people separate geographically from each other and can no longer communicate in person.

Today the authorities in China seem to be attempting to create a more populist alphabetic version of the written form of the language that would bring all outlying provinces into one educational and, it is hoped, political embrace. The reality is still complicated. If two persons, one from Mukden in Manchuria, the other from Chonquing in Szechwan, read the same Mandarin text orally to each other, they would hear mutually unintelligible material.

A similar phenomenon can happen in the United States. Listen to speakers from Alabama, Massachusetts, and Oklahoma. Unless it is anchored, as English is, in an alphabetic version of an originating form of the language, such as the King's English, writing can, as it has in China, reflect quite different phonological/sound versions from one part of the nation to other distant geographies.

## HEARING THE ALPHABET

The alphabetic form of our language does require of parents and teachers certain child-rearing and teaching awareness. First, we must remember that each child is eventually going to make a transition from being an exclusively speaking and listening language user. This will require that she become at least as competent in the alternate, more abstract language skills: reading and writing.

We might name this transitional stage in the learning-to-read process "readiness." Simply put, the child at this stage becomes self-consciously aware of the meaningful sounds of the words and sentences that she is both speaking herself and hearing from other speakers. These sounds might technically be called the *phonological structure* of spoken English.

The skills are simple to describe, and there are a multitude of exercises and games that parents and teachers can create to greatly increase the child's self-consciousness about this sound structure of her language. We want the child to be able to distinguish the sounds of letters and their combinations as they are formed into words and sentences. It is important that the child hear herself say these words and distinguish the different sounds, and implicitly, *if not yet*, the letters that represent these sounds, for these are the visual symbols that will become written words.

The child should also be able to hear differences in the constituent sounds when parents, teachers, or other adults speak. For example, the parent could ask the child if she can tell the differences in the beginning sounds of the words "mommy" and "nanny" or "popsicle" and "buckle," or the final sounds of words such as "luck" and "man" or "dad" and "bag." Such games can also be played with middle sounds in easy words. Always, it is important for children to repeat and thus hear the sounds and the words as they themselves pronounce them.

**Table 2.2**
**Components of a Sound-Based Language**

| | |
|---|---|
| **PHONEMES** | The individual sound units that our language chooses to emphasize. |
| **MORPHEMES** | The smallest meaningful units of a word, whose combination creates a word. Plurals are morphemes. |
| **SYNTAX** | The admissible combinations of words in phrases and sentences (called grammar, in popular usage). |
| **SEMANTICS** | The meanings that correspond to all lexical items and to all possible sentences. Children read for meaning. |
| **LEXICON** | The collection of all words in a given language. Each lexical entry includes all information with morphological or syntactic ramifications but does not include conceptual knowledge. |
| **PROSODY** | The vocal intonation that can modify the literal meaning of words and sentences. |
| **DISCOURSE** | The linking of sentences such that they constitute a narrative. Paragraphs lead to stories: fact or fiction. |

Games can be played with digraphs such as "ch" and "sh" as in "chin" and "shin"; "gh" as in "tough"; "ph" as in "phone"; "th" as in "thing" or "this." The point is that the child should be able to hear differences that the parent or teacher sees as important for the later awareness of the irregularity of the language. Rules should not be imposed. Neither is it necessary at this stage to expose actual written materials to a child who is not yet ready to perceive and distinguish the visual differences in letters and what they stand for in the phonology—the sounds.

Above all, remember: Do these learning activities with the child in an informal manner. Play games, make up contests, always stimulating the child to greater awareness. You are the only one who needs to know that this is all part of a long-range "plot" to help her become a quick learner and reader.

The principle is that the child should be prepared eventually to handle a phonetic or *mediated* introduction to the skill of reading. It is a rare child who will later succeed in even a modest introduction to what is called *inductive phonics*—phonics without rules— without first being able to hear the sounds and distinguish them, from the standpoint of listening to her own speech and that of others.

On the other hand, some children will learn to read without being excellent "sound-distinguishing" types. These are children whose visual systems—what lies behind the eyes in terms of neurologically connected wiring to the language and reading system and the "thinking brain"—are primed for reading. For various reasons, this type of quick fluent reader is not found as often as in the heyday of the look-say, sight approach to reading.

But this type of purely visual reader does exist in some numbers, and parents should not be overly upset if their child is not a good "hearer" of sound differences in speech. This is one of the reasons that parents ought to be prepared for the upcoming confrontation with actual reading long before it is scheduled to occur. They should be mentally prepared for all the variations that are possible in their own child's learning.

As we will point out later, the very nature of achieving fluency in reading allows many different approaches to getting beyond surface skills and down into the "deep structure" of understanding. Making the phonetic transition from speaking and hearing to seeing, reading, and knowing, as I have explained above, can be mobilized by many different teaching and learning strategies. Parents and teachers need to have all of them at the ready.

the text, develops context understandings. The child learns that in that hodge-podge of black on white is a story, somewhat like the stories that Dad tells at bedtime, but steadier and simpler in its variation of words and nuances. In its many rereadings, the story will become part of the child's world of imaginative experiences. And she will crave for ever more new ones.

After several years of being read to, healthy normal children begin to develop a taste for independence in getting at the fascinating people and events that exist within the covers of their books. Make sure they know that one of these days, "You, too, will be able to read about *Yogurt and the Crystal Snowman* and all his friends." The anticipation will constitute a powerful motivational force when the child finally enters the reading classroom.

It is a good idea for the preschool or kindergarten child to know about newspapers and magazines, and the various print sources for reading. What of all the print material on television, especially ads? These should be read by adults to the child as they pass over the screen. Because there is so much repetition in these ads, children will begin to recognize the shape of the words in association with the pictures of the items on the screen. This can be a good first step for some children who, it is sad to say, opportunely have learned to "break the code" through the over-viewed "idiot box."

## Letter Names and Their Sounds

Parents should try to observe their child's readiness to perceive the relationship between an easy consonant sound and the letter that typically represents the sound, "m" for "mommy," "b" for "boat," or "p" for "pear," usually coordinated with the pictured equivalent. One never can predict the developmental readiness of the child. This means that the parent should try out all sorts of combinations and little fun "tricks" with their child.

The key parental discipline lies in not being too eager, and not pushing too hard. Children will show their readiness, especially if they are surrounded by print in books, magazines, newspapers, and appropriate computer games. If the child displays no interest in or sensitivity to the distinctions in letter shapes, their sounds, and the simple words that utilize these sounds, the rule must be: Lay off—absolutely.

**Figure 3.1**
**Auditory Discrimination/Initial Consonants**

**Figure 3.1** (continued)

### Subtest 4   Auditory Discrimination/Initial Consonants (pages 9–10)

Open your booklet to page 9. [Give help as necessary.] On this page you will listen for beginning sounds.

**Sample row**

Find the picture of the cat at the top of the page. [Point to the cat at the top of your booklet.] The cat means I will help you with this row.

Look at the picture of the boy next to the cat. [Point to the boy.] Listen as I say its name: *boy.* [Stress the initial consonant sound in *boy.*] In this row we are going to look for another picture whose name begins with the same sound as *boy.*

Look at the other pictures in the row. Listen as I say their names: *puzzle, balloon, van.* The words *puzzle* and *van* do not begin with the same sound as *boy.* Does the word *balloon* begin with the same sound as *boy?* Yes, it does.

Draw a line under the picture of the balloon to show that it begins with the same sound as *boy.* [Demonstrate. Wait.]

[Point to the underlined picture of the balloon.] If you did not draw a line under this picture of a balloon, do it now. Erase any other marks you have made. [Check that all pupils have drawn a line under the picture of the balloon before continuing.]

**Item 27**

Now move down to the next row. Point to the next row just as I am. [Demonstrate and check.] Look at the picture I am pointing to. [Point to the girl.] Listen as I say its name: *girl.* [Stress the initial consonant sound in *girl.*]

Now listen as I say the names of the other pictures in the row: *goat, table, bone.* Draw a line under the picture whose name begins with the same sound as *girl.*

**Items 28–31**

[Continue in the same way for the remaining items on the page. Tell pupils to find and point to each row. Point to it in your booklet. The following are the first pictures to point to and name and the other pictures to name for each row.]
28. *key: belt, king, house*
29. *top: tire, man, bell*
30. *mitten: kite, mouse, rooster*
31. *fork: bed, pencil, fish*

*Source*: "Reading Readiness" by R. L. Allington. Reprinted by permission of HarperCollins College Publishers.

Try again in a few weeks, always casually and without heavy emotional or disciplinary involvement. The family motto should be *relax*—this should be a game that carries no great burden of success or failure. Eventually, rarely at three, sometimes at four, more often at five or beyond, the child will begin to demonstrate awareness of the differences between the "z" of "zebra" and the "c" of "cat," both visually and through sound.

As these developmental awarenesses begin to show up in the child's heightening interest in letters and their sounds, the parent might begin to show the child that the letters not only have unique shapes and sounds, but that they also have names. It is not a bad idea to do as teachers in their classrooms always do, paper the child's bedroom or playroom with examples of the letters, their names, and most common picture/sounds that they represent, perhaps even the words that represent—the "a" of "apple," or the "d" of "dog."

Parents will find workbooks or computer programs that give the child practice in visual discrimination of shapes, different arrangement of sails on a boat, more abstract combinations of geometrical lines and circles, even pseudo-words, to test their awareness of similarities and differences: "Which one of these four pictures is the same as the example; which one is different from the others?"

Be careful with this latter test of discriminatory awareness of visual differences and similarities in shapes and forms. For, to be sensitive to the twenty-six different letters in the English language, especially each having some kind of concrete sound equivalency, requires a much smaller critical visual discriminatory sense than is tested for in so-called "performance" testing, such as in IQ tests. Letter differences are easier to discern by the five- or six-year-old than most of the abstract shapes that appear on tests and games.

Also, these tests carry a much higher burden of success and failure than is required in the letter and word recognition phases of a child learning to read. Often such visual skills in discrimination and recognition have little predictive power when it comes to fluent reading mastery.

Experience tells us that to recognize the visual differences in letters and the words that comprise letter combinations does not require extraordinary visual discriminatory powers. The kinds of testing and work materials that are useful for guiding four- and five-year-olds through such visual discriminatory development stages are fairly simple. However, they do comprise a crucial hurdle in the development of readiness for reading.


## Words and Meanings

On traditional readiness tests, such as the *Metropolitan*, published by Harcourt, two tests dip into the child's ordinary awareness of language and the outside world to which it applies. One, entitled "Word Meaning," gives a series of line drawings, three for each question. For example, there might be pictures of three different nuts: an acorn, a walnut, and a chestnut. The teacher will ask the children to put an "x" on the picture of the walnut (after demonstrating how to do this). Another example might show drawings of a bird in flight, a duck, and a shoe-like object, with the child being asked to mark the moccasin.

What this test attempts to discover is, simply, the child's awareness at five-and-a-half to six years of age of the relationship of things in the world to the language that humans apply to this world. It is developmentally and educationally revealing to note the level of experience or, sadly, deprivation of the child. It could also be an augury of intellectual difficulties to come if such simple tests reveal a child incapable of making many of these relational judgments.

The next test in the *Metropolitan* is called "Listening." After the usual demonstration as to how to mark the test booklet, making sure that all the children understand the directions, the teacher begins. In one of the earliest of the examples, the teacher reads: "In Switzerland the cows wear bells around their necks so the boy can find them when they wander away. Mark the picture that shows this." In the other two drawings, one shows a boy half reclining with his dog beside him, the other a group of four sheep.

One of the more difficult examples, at the end of the test, is phrased as follows: "While Mother got the money ready, the clerk tied up her package. Mark the picture that shows that." In the other two drawings, one shows a clerk ringing up items on the register, the other a group of packages without a human figure.

Clearly, this is a comprehension test that links the ability to observe picture events with the ability to discern their differences, then to choose the picture event that matches the teacher's description. Experienced educators do not draw long-term or profound conclusions on the basis of such testing. What we are observing in the child is her readiness to engage in the kinds of learning that are typical and average for children in the five- to six-year-old age range.

An even more intriguing readiness test is the one devoted to number concepts. There are twenty-six examples in this test, of which the first is a teacher demonstration to ensure that all the children understand what they are to do. To exemplify what these five- to six-year-old youngsters are challenged with, I will paraphrase the instructions for three examples. The test usually gives the child four choices. One asks the child to look at four similar houses having different numbers of windows. The child will be asked to mark the house, for example, that has five windows. Next the child will be asked to look at a row of pencils. The question could be, if the child had three pencils and Mother gave her four more, to put an X on the picture that shows how many pencils the child now has. In the final example, the child is asked to mark the number that means more than 42 but fewer than 56. The proper number to be marked would be 52.

It should be apparent that parents who concentrate solely on instructing their children in the ordinal numbers—the sequence 1 through 10, for example—are not really facing up to the meaning of number concepts as exemplified in this reading readiness test. Here the children are challenged to think conceptually, to understand the relationships embodied in the idea of *quantity*.

What does this have to do with reading and reading readiness? Plenty. When educators study the success or failure of children in making their way through common reading programs, they find that sometimes in second grade, when the children should have gone beyond the beginning stages and on to the threshold of fluent reading or even into fast comprehension, considering the second-grade types of reading material, it is the number test, of all the readiness tests, that most precisely predicts this later success or failure in reading!

Why is this? As I will attempt to explain later on, success in fluent reading and comprehension ultimately has little to do with visual or auditory perception, and much to do with understanding, predicting, and organizing the seemingly visual inputs of the graphic reading material into a dynamic web of meaning expectations. This web of meaning the child has within her brain.

The number test, of all the tests in the *Metropolitan* battery, is the most purely cognitive—it is a thinking test.

Naturally, all these comments are tempered by the fact that children at this age level vary enormously in their developmental readiness. The variation is especially noticeable between girls and boys, the boys usually lagging behind the girls in maturity.

## CONFUSION ROAD

### Perceptual/Motor and Sensory Development

There is a commonly held view that the pathway toward reading fluency is an upward sequential process. This view can be persuasive and seemingly logical, but it is truly erroneous. It holds that since reading is the ultimate intellectual step that children will make in their education, it must be preceded and prepared for by the mastery of certain developmentally simpler and prior physical, sensory, and perceptual skill accomplishments.

As Dr. Maria Montessori phrased it, "Reading . . . requires a much longer course of instruction and . . . calls for a superior intellectual development, since it treats of the *interpretation of signs*, and of the *modulation of accents of the voice*, in order that the word may be understood. And all this is a purely mental task, while in writing, the child, under dictation, *materially translates* sounds into signs, and *moves* a thing which is always easy and pleasant for him. Writing develops in the little child—with *facility* and *spontaneity*, analogous to the spoken language which is a motor translation of audible sounds. Reading, on the contrary, makes part of an abstract intellectual culture, which is the interpretation of ideas from graphic symbols, and is only acquired later on."[1]

These ideas were originally expressed in the Italian version of Montessori's book, published in 1909. Therefore, the psychological perspective expressed here is now quite out of date. But in its influence on educational practice, especially as applied to the early years of learning, it has been continuously applied.

Montessori Schools, wherever they are found in the world, and, to a lesser or greater extent, other devout followers of this distinguished educational pioneer, tend to utilize many of the materials, and provide the moral and psychological environment that Montessori produced in her "Casa di Bambini," established for Roman slum children, who, at the least, were severely deprived socially, and often psychologically.

This is why in the above quote we can see Montessori's preference that writing precede reading for five-year-olds. Writing is physical as Montessori puts it, a "motor translation." Montessori's view of the proper developmental sequence of learning for the child requires control first over "material reality."

This means that before one attends to a more intellectual confrontation with the abstract signs of reading, which Montessori erroneously tends to reduce to being a reproduction of speech (more on that later), one must be sure that the child masters these preparatory physical steps.

These steps involve the traditional sensory and motor development skills outlined in the more American-oriented Orton-Gillingham method, which integrates motor functioning and sensory awareness skills as both diagnosis of future problems and preparation for reading. Children should be able to discern color differences and reproduce geometrical shapes such as circles, squares, and triangles, for both recognition and actual physical constructions.

The Montessori method includes an enormous amount of good physical and perceptual training. The children compare sizes and reproduce physical arrangements in special design boxes after observing and then taking them apart. They learn to distinguish left from right, do exercises that call upon them to understand laterality by actually acting out exercises with left or right in varying sequences. In general, this sequential approach is viewed as developmentally necessary, requiring that one phase be completed before the child is allowed to proceed to the next.

The criterion for reading in all the varieties of sensory-motor training lies less in linguistic materials than it does in distinguishing: discerning levels of smoothness from roughness and round shapes from oblongs, and being able to recognize what size object can fit into what size inset.

Don't we all know that before a child walks, the child crawls, then toddles? Is it not true that the development of the child proceeds from the concrete materiality and physicality of experience to increasingly intellectual tasks? Reading being the most abstract of learnings, it should not take place until the child has moved successfully through all the prerequisite sensory/material, perceptual/motor skills.

Good facts? Yes. Good reasoning? *No!*

As an example, most children crawl before they walk. It is developmentally to be expected, but it is not always the case. Certainly the human sequence of physical development suggests this sequence. Reading as a developmental process in the maturation of the child, however, works off of a separate neurological system from the physical muscular, sensory, and motor structures of our development. It is a language skill that evolves in often surprisingly different sequences from the sensory/motor system.

Not only does reading evolve as part of children's language development independent of their physical maturation, but it often develops independently in time and strength as compared to their speaking and listening skills.

On the basis of the assumption that sensory/motor development and language intellectual development are linked in a causal manner, and that we need to perfect the first before we can teach the latter, one would expect that the truly phenomenal basketball players that we view on television would be linguistic virtuosos as well. On the basis of their television interviews, this is clearly not the case. How well, then, have they learned to read?

One of the most decisive refutations of the idea that language and reading skills are dependent on the maturation of motor and sensory development is the documented fact that many perfectly coordinated children, appropriate candidates for such a badge of readiness, have difficulty learning to read regardless of the methods of reading instruction intended for normal children. On the other hand, a myriad of children—stumblers, gawky, and awkward—have no difficulty at all in learning to read fluently.

A good theory of the reading process have to make predictions about what will happen and/or not happen if we apply its tenets. Montessori, Orton-Gillingham, and other sensory, perceptual, motor approaches don't always work as they claim. They, therefore, fail to help us understand and assist the reading/learning process.

## NOTE

1. Maria Montessori. 1912, 1964. *The Montessori Method.* New York: Schocken, 226–267.

# Chapter 4

# *Slow Reading: Phonics and Decoding*

**PHONICS?**

Eventually, the preliminaries must end. The child is aging. She is now six years old and entering first grade. Soon she will be looking at her first reading book and its stories. Now is the time for the teacher to begin a systematic reading program. Such a program should continue well beyond first grade, up into the middle years.

While the parents are at home holding their breath—for they instinctively know how crucial reading is to the educational future of their child—the television lights up, loaded with hope. There is a commercial for a new video phonics program to help children at home master beginning reading. How fortuitous, and it has a money-back guarantee for *x* days in case you are not satisfied or change your mind.

There are many such programs, including the "Hooked on Phonics" program espoused and sponsored by various corporations. Each takes advantage of the great discontent of the American people over the general state of literacy in our country, but far more important, the increasing percentage of children who learn to read only with great difficulty, and who ever after, if not hating to read, resist it and turn on the television set.

No serious objection can be raised to such panaceas, *except* and ✓ *unless. Except* means that usually the claims—and the federal government in 1994 agreed—made by the "Hooked on Phonics" people were out of line with reality. They withdrew to more modest assertions.

The qualification *unless* carries a big hesitation, for the parent as well the teacher must understand what phonics can do for the child, as well as do *to* the child. And we state this qualification, that the most positive benefits of phonics cannot be guaranteed *unless* it is taught under the best educational conditions.

The discouraging part of the present stage in the seemingly perennial reading wars is that both the advocates as well as the enemies of phonics as part of beginning reading instruction deal only in extremes. They are either totally "for" phonics as the cure-all for the evils that professional educators have inflicted on beginning readers, or, as with most of the reading profession, having transferred their allegiance from "look-say," the sight method, to whole language, view phonics with unrestrained snobbish disdain.

✓ Phonics can be a crude simplification of what should be a rich literate experience for the child. Yet few classroom programs in beginning reading, in first grade, or even earlier in kindergarten or preschool, will have completely ignored the phonics element of visual language development. It still works its way into the classroom, as well it should. Few children can do without some steady exposure to the phonics experience, and that exposure should take place over many months of conscientious teaching.

There are two basic questions regarding the teaching of beginning reading through phonics: (1) Is the teacher aware that phonics is only a brief way-station on the road to true or fluent reading? and (2) Does the curricular program that the school and classroom present to your child embody a proper understanding as to what phonics can do for the child, and what it should not attempt to do?

## PHONICS NOW SEEMS IMPORTANT

There was time, well over fifty years ago, when a large percentage of American children learned to read from a purely sight approach, through the so-called controlled vocabulary. The children were shown common and easy words and they listened to the words as spoken by the teacher. As she spoke the words, the teacher ran her pointer over the shapes of the letters. Only rarely did she launch into a "sounding-out" description of the words. Perhaps she assumed that the mere speaking of the word in association with its visual graphic expression, usually with an appropriate picture of the dog, Spot, or the young girl, Jane, was enough to make the learning point.

Since the publication of *Why Johnny Can't Read* by Rudolf Flesch in 1955, the American public has become aware that something has gone wrong with Johnny's as well as Judy's reading success. Phonics has made a great comeback, at the behest of concerned parents as well as media and political groups that consider themselves watchdogs of the education profession.

Something definitely went wrong. As we will point out in the next chapter, the basic principle of the sight approach is, however, not that far wrong. A teacher can do much less harm to the child through the sight approach than through the phonics approach. In the first case, the teacher will have to start at the beginning to assist a child who is completely unable to "get it." In the latter instance, a teacher may spend more time undoing the crippling impact of poor teaching on the child's ability to read than it would have taken to start from scratch. Too often, the debilitating effects of phonics are not noted until it is too late to mend the damage.

One view of the failure of the sight approach is that teachers became too casual about putting children into a systematic program of instruction. One opinion has it that progressive education's child-centered, lackadaisical attitude toward systematic learning simply missed on many children who cried out for careful day-by-day instructional supervision.

Another hypothesis is that the student population in our schools has changed. Today's children seem to need much more help on their way into fluent reading—rapid encoding of the visual letters and words into meaning—than did the children of previous generations. Couple this with the fact that those children who missed out on learning to read in the old days often slid through the net and went into the world where they had to fend for themselves. And they were often successful.

In today's heavily print-oriented society, it is no longer possible to exist within the worldwide economic community without being a competent reader. We notice our failures more now than we did before, mainly because we are forced to.

## USEFULNESS FOR YOUR CHILD

For the purposes of this discussion, we assume that your child is typical. She needs some phonics exposure in a systematic reading program as she matures neurologically to the point that she can begin not merely to decode words to their spoken equivalents, but also to encode words and sentences directly into meaning.

Let us present some of the variations that we will find in children. Otherwise, the "typical" child remains an enigma.

The easiest "problem" for both teacher and parent are those vanishing "natural" readers who need few phonics clues. They can watch television, see the ads and logos, hear the Pepsis and Cokes pronounced and displayed, see words in picture magazines and children's books that are read to them by parents. They are presented with all the obvious clues indicated above and others that their curious minds pick out of their daily experiences. Here and there, a few questions are asked of parent or teachers.

Then, picking up clues from the likes of "cat," "mat," "rat," and "fat," they get the idea and begin to read on their own. Yes, they will make errors when they are reading aloud. Often, the errors are what we call meaning miscues—"Jack and Jill *walked* up the hill" instead of "Jack and Jill *ran* up the hill.— They get the point of reading—encoding the print directly into meaning—but do not bother to look as carefully as they should. Sometimes, as in the middle grades, they will mispronounce a word—pronounce "hyperbole" as "hipperbowl"—that they understand from the context of their reading but have never heard spoken. No problem here.

Others in the group may have various, often mysterious, problems. They may be physically and neurologically immature. They could be uninterested in school, or bullied at home to learn when they are not ready. Some have real reading disabilities-in-the-making. They desperately need a slow, systematic course of learning to read, especially if in preschool and kindergarten no diagnostic assessment was made, for which a reading readiness program is an essential prerequisite.

In reality, what most children need is the true beginning of all reading in an alphabetical language. This takes place in the slow transition from the spoken sounds of the natural language to as similar as possible a print replication of these sounds. This can take place and be taught in a simple phonics instructional program. Such an approach might not be too different from many of the new commercial print and television offerings, including many of the techniques illustrated on such children's television programs as Sesame Street, or in the magazine of the same name.

We want the child not merely to decode the visual graphemes (letters), to their sound equivalents, but also to create words and sentences out of them. After all, we read to gain meaning from print, not merely to hear the sounds embedded in the letter combinations. Phonics instructions should give the child the easiest version of the regularity in sight to sound that exists in our written English.

"Baby will cry for mama" might be an example of a sentence that the child could sound out letter by letter, slowly, then word by word. As she becomes skilled in doing this kind of decoding task, it would be quite possible for the child to reach the end of the sentence *before* she forgets what was in the first part. She therefore could gain an elementary level of comprehension.

But we must remember that the phonics approach to reading—decoding the letters and words to sound and then listening to what has been read either orally or subvocally—requires a final step by the child. She must then place the spoken equivalents of the written symbols into her mind for understanding. When we speak and listen to each other, we do this automatically. We "understand" virtually simultaneously as we hear each other.

Phonics decoding to sound and then to words and meaning is not instantaneous. Either listen to a five- or six-year-old read by this process or try to mimic this approach as an adult, and you will readily understand the basic drawback. It is *slow* going. Too often, the child will forget the words at the beginning of the sentence before she has finished decoding to the end, and therefore lose the general meaning of the entire sentence.

This is because of a basic neurological and brain peculiarity in humans called short-term memory. It is different from long-term memory, in which practically all our lifetime's knowledge is embedded. Here, in long-term memory, exist some of those experiences and memories that psychoanalysts have attempted to plumb and retrieve for us so that we may understand ourselves more deeply.

Short-term memory is what we need when we try to remember small bits of unrelated material, such as telephone numbers. Lists of names or numbers, anything without a structure of meaning on which to hang our memory hats, must struggle with the capacity limitations of short-term memory. That is why to memorize things like names and numbers, we often have to run around our apartment or office rehearsing such bits of information until we have written them down. Or we associate them in our minds with our favorite ice cream flavor or the address of our parents.

When a child reads a meaningful word or sentence and understands it, her short-term memory, as in a lifted magic writing page, is renewed, after which she can now store additional memory items. It is passed into long-term memory and understanding. But for a child using phonics, using this slow step-by-step process of accumulating information, letter sounds, and their elaboration into words, takes time. It *has* to slow the child down.

As noted in the Introduction, a little over 100 years ago, James Cattell, a psychologist at Columbia University, returned from Germany, where he had done graduate work on the nature of human memory. He applied what he had learned there to the construction of the tachistoscope. The tachistoscope helped us to understand why we seemed to be able to remember instantaneously, in the same small fraction of a second, five letters or five words (20–25 letters), sometimes even five sentences (80–90 letters) that were flashed on a screen.

The principle here is that the mind looks for *meaning*. Letters grouped into words or sentences provide meaning. The mind therefore ignores the component twenty-five, or even eighty letters and "chunks" them swiftly into meaning.

Phonics decoding, slowing as it does our visual absorption of print, therefore limits the amount of material that can be stored in short-term memory, often just a few letters, because it does not invoke our mind and its need to find sense in what it sees.

On the other hand, phonics as a beginning reading tool is useful because of its assistance to that majority of children who will need additional maturity, instruction, and guidance in moving into the more natural and fluent stage of reading. These children need more time in getting the "idea" of reading as searching, amid all the letters and sounds, for the meanings that lie beneath the visual surface appearances of print. Phonics reading may be slow, but it can be a useful tool that can lead gradually to greater speed of reading and the automatic transmission of simple reading material to deeper comprehension.

**Table 4.1**
**More Meaning: More Letters Identified**

---

1. $P$ $T$ $F$ $L$ $G$ ⟨ S T N R Q ⟩ $F$ $L$ $X$ $M$ $U$ $B$

We remember four or five random letters.

2. A B O U T ⟨ R U N N E R  G O N E ⟩ F O R  B R A T

We remember two words of about ten letters.

3. D O G S  B I T E  H U M A N S  W H E N  A N G R Y

We remember a meaningful statement of about twenty-five letters.

---

In one glance, we remember more letters that have meaning.

## MISTAKEN BELIEF

Much that has been written about phonics as the sure road to effective reading is based on a false belief. This idea is that written language as exemplified in English is derived from speech, or more colloquially, print is *written-down speech.*

There is no question that without speech there would be no writing. But writing and reading do not automatically follow from the fact of speech, which is universal among all human beings. Writing is a system of communicating ideas and emotions, as is speech, but it is rooted in different systems of brain function. It is certainly not as basic to the structure of human behavior as is speech, which issues from vocal and other neurological functions that we can trace back to our ancestors, the apes and monkeys.

Recall that the Chinese system of writing and reading also originates in the spoken language—classical Mandarin Chinese. Over the centuries, as the different geographical sections of China went their own ways culturally, which occurred likewise within the spoken language (considering the fluid and ever-changing character of all spoken dialects), people began to read the classical script with very different sound equivalents. If written language were merely transcribed vocalizations, this would not have been possible.

In our own country, where the dialects are not as different from each other as compared with those in China, first-graders from Texas and Vermont, respectively, have no trouble understanding the same beginning readers. They may speak differently and pronounce their vowels and blends oddly, but even with their very different dialects, they can reach more easily than the Chinese the same understanding of the meaning of the Dick, Jane, and Sally stories.

Also, as I will point out below, the enormous irregularities in the English language as to how to pronounce various words, given their often contradictory spellings, patently falsifies the claim that there is more than only a rough congruence between the sounds of our speech, whatever our accents, and the written version of the language.

It comes back to the theme enunciated in Chapter 2 of this book, that the problem of literacy, in children as well as adults, is related to the fact that there is language by ear as well as language by eye. Language by eye is indeed derived from the prior biological existence of language by ear. But the written form of our language is basically an intellectually created code, which as noted above with regard to Chinese *logography* or even the picture writing of the early civilizations, is derived from but does not mimic speech.

## NO-RULES PHONICS

At one time in the history of the wars over the teaching of reading, systematic phonics instruction was seen as the pathway to long-term reading competency. In the struggle in the late 1950s over the direction of educational reform, the alliance of the sight approach to reading with professional educators and their very liberal political allies caused the shape of reading reform to be influenced by noneducational, that is, political considerations.

The connection of phonics with traditional one-room schoolhouse teaching patterns fitted the sharply conservative political tenor of that period. The result was a series of claims about phonics and reading that went further than anything heretofore seen in the educational literature.[1]

In fact, since the advent of psycholinguistic theory and the various writings of its advocates, the claims for phonics have been steadily demeaned. Rarely in the professional literature does one now see the once-exuberant puffing by phonics advocates.

The 1950s and 1960s represent an era of teaching phonics by rules—what the written symbols of letters and combinations of letters sound like. It was thought that the child could utilize these rules to decode new and previously unseen words—the "a" in "apple" would help the child read the "a"in "cat"; the "sh" in "rush" would assist in decoding the "sh" in "bush."

Or course, there were the many exceptions: the "gh" in "cough" would never work in "thought." The "th" in "this" would sound different in "thistle." The exceptions would go on forever. Linguists began to examine this fascinating irregularity in our language, partially the result of so many historical overlaying linguistic incursions. In our English homeland, we added Scandinavian to the indigenous Anglo-Saxon. Then, French was added, with its ancient classical roots together with smatterings of even earlier and more esoteric traditions.

In the early 1970s, it was already understood that our basic twenty-six-letter alphabet, if it included sounds represented by more than one letter, "ou," "th," and "ng," for instance, consisted of at least fifty-two major spelling units; thirty-two consonant units and twenty vowels. Further research identified 211 different ways that spelling units—"gh," "oy," and "ch," as in "ghost," "ploy," and "rich,"— could be related to different soundings of similar spellings—"ph" as in "telephone" and "haphazard."

Out of this study came 166 basic rules. Even with all the rules, approximately 10 percent of the words that six- to nine-year-old children come across in their reading in the first years of schooling, over 6,000 one- and two-syllable words, were still exceptions to the 166 rules.

It should be obvious that no ordinary child should be forced into that endless tunnel of rules and exceptions. Just imagine what happens to children who are attempting to work their way through a sentence using systematic phonics, even with some efficiency. They must struggle against time through the sentence, before their short-term memory gives out. Then they have to bring to the front of their minds rules that were memorized earlier.

**Table 4.2**
**Rule-Based Phonics: Conformance Percentages**

| Rule | Words Conforming | Exceptions | Percent Conforming to Rule |
|---|---|---|---|
| 1. When there are two vowels side by side, the long sound of the first one is heard and the second is usually silent. | 309 (bead) | 377 (chief) | 45 |
| 2. When a vowel is in the middle of a one-syllable word, the vowel is short. | 408 | 249 | 62 |
| middle letter | 191 (dress) | 84 (scold) | 69 |
| one of the middle two letters in a word of four letters | 191 (rest) | 135 (told) | 59 |
| one vowel *within* a word of more than four letters | 26 (splash) | 30 (fight) | 46 |
| 3. If the only vowel letter is at the end of a word the letter usually stands for a long sound. | 23 (he) | 8 (to) | 74 |
| 4. When there are two vowels, one of which is final *e*, the first vowel is long and the *e* is silent. | 180 (bone) | 108 (done) | 63 |
| 5. The *r* gives the preceding vowel a sound that is neither long nor short. | 484 (horn) | 134 (wire) | 78 |
| 6. The first vowel is usually long and the second silent in the diagraphs *ai, ea, oa,* and *ui.* | 179 | 92 | 66 |
| ai | 43 (nail) | 24 (said) | 64 |
| ea | 101 (bead) | 51 (head) | 66 |
| oa | 34 (boat) | 1 (cupboard) | 97 |
| ui | 1 (suit) | 16 (build) | 6 |

**Table 4.3**
**Examples of Exceptions to Phonics "Rules"**

---

### Consonant-Vowel-Consonant (CVC) Clusters:

| | | | |
|---|---|---|---|
| a | bad, dad, glad | star, far, car, | what |
| | cat, sat, fat | call, tall, wall | was |
| | back, sack, tack | bank, sank, thank | wand |
| | bag, rag, tag | bang, hang, sang | war |
| | can, ran, man | | |
| | cap, map, tap | | |
| | ash, cash, mash | | |
| | last, fast, mast | | |
| | band, strand, land | | |
| e | bed, led, red | her | |
| | set, met, get | fern | |
| | less, mess, chess | | |
| | pen, hen, ten | | |
| | send, bend, end | | |
| | nest, best, rest | | |
| | neck, deck, peck | | |
| | bent, sent, tent | | |
| i | bin, pin, tin | sir | pint |
| | chip, tip, lip | hill, mill, bill | sign |
| | bit, fit, hit | mind, kind, rind | |
| | dip, rip, skip | fight, tight, light | |
| | dish, fish, wish | child, mild | |
| | sick, pick, tick | | |
| | ink, think, mink | | |
| o | hop, chop, drop | for | clothes |
| | pot, got, hot | roll, toll, troll | off |
| | clock, dock, rock | most, post, ghost | won |
| | | cold, hold, told | worn |
| | | song, long, gong | |
| u | mug, bug, rug | fun | pull |
| | sun, fun, run | hurt | truth |
| | duck, truck, luck | dull, hull, skull | |
| | junk, sunk, trunk | | |

---

### Consonant-Vowel-Consonant-Silent E (CV and CVCe) Clusters:

| | | | |
|---|---|---|---|
| a/e | ate, gate, skate | care, bare, dare | have |
| | gave, cave, save | tale, pale, sale | are |
| | cake, bake, lake | | dance |
| | plane, cane, mane | | |
| | same, lame, tame | | |
| e/e | he, me, we | here | fence |
| | these | were | |
| | | there | |
| i/e | fine, mine, nine | tire, fire, hire | give |
| | bike, like, hike | pile, smile, file | since |
| | hide, wide, slide | | |

---

Not only are they trying to read the meaning of the words they are attempting to decode to sound, but they are also thinking about the rules that apply as they sound out. We now know that to sound out, no matter how many sure-fire rules the child learns, the unique meaning of the word will define the sounded-out pronunciation.

Note that the above tedious regimen is what is required of a young six-year-old novice reader using the pedagogical rules of systematic phonics. The reality is that for a truly fluent reader, the process of going from sight to meaning should be rapid and automatic. For the child taught solely through systematic phonics instruction, the only result can be memory breakdown and mental fatigue, and ultimately, revulsion for the reading experience.

We will explain in greater detail in the next chapter how the automatic reading system operates, unknown to the child, in a subliminal manner. Here, encoding from the visual-neurological level directly into meaning is aided by speed of reading. If a child has to remember rules for each of the letters and combinations, then all the exceptions to the rules, her comprehension, indeed the decoding process itself, has to come to a frustrating halt.

In summary, this approach, through the so-called "rules of phonetic decoding," constitutes a pathway of destruction for children's hopes of becoming successful and happy fluent readers.

What, then, is the alternative, if we utilize what is functional in the phonics approach? The answer is: *No* spoken rules, only silently displayed examples and exceptions. Say to the child: "Here is the word 'bird.' The letter 'b' [point] is what we hear at the beginning of the word 'bird.' Do you see the picture in the book? What is it?" Exceptional or unusual combinations can be shown to the child without the expression of a rule. Most children will catch on after a very few examples as to what the usual sound of a "b" or a "d" as well as the several sounds of "a," "u," "c," and "th."

What is the advantage of giving the commonalities of the sound/sight relationships to children through examples without asking them to remember "rules"? The advantage is that children will internalize what the teacher shows them, and create personal dictionaries in their sight/sound language/reading system. These "dictionaries" inside each child's mind will spontaneously lead to pronunciation decisions that children will make in their beginning oral reading. Thus, they *do not* have to involve the conscious thinking, rule-observing part of the brain.

Cognition or long-term memory lies deep in our minds. It takes tangible seconds to reactivate and be brought up for use in acting out a decision that leads to a specific behavior. It is a little like walking, running, or riding a bike. Sometimes the body and mind learn to do something in a way that the thinking brain can inhibit or foul up if we think about it too much.

In the case of "no-rules phonics," we should show the child as many of these correlations between sight and sound as are reasonable over a delimited instructional time period, having fun with the exceptions, and leaving it at that. The child's own neurology will take over and create her personal dictionary, her spontaneously activated memory bank of reading correlations. As she reads, these inner relationships will be activated momentarily, and without the necessity for intellectual analysis, well before short-term memory surrenders its brief gasp of connectivity.

At least, we hope and expect that this will happen to the child. We want to avoid any barriers that might block the child's gradual transition into what we call visual or featural reading, which will be explained in the next chapter. Again, remember that for some children, phonics suggestibility will be an only momentary clue leading to the real thing taking place in the *reading system*.

For others, who are immature in a diverse number of developmental ways, patient, subtle, and steady phonics exposure, along with other teaching approaches, including sight word recognition skills and word analysis, taking words apart and putting them back together, may prepare them for their reading breakthrough. The rule for parents and teachers is to serve a rich repertoire of language skill development experiences, expecting that ever-wonderful "magic moment."

Some will not experience this magic moment of transition to fluent reading. But we must never stop searching for the cause or causes of any child's reading failure. Specialists in diagnostic reading or clinical analysis, or even, as a last resort, specialists in intelligence testing, can be consulted. Testing may reveal different learning modality preferences in such children, for example, for a few, the primacy of the sense of touch. The key here is to probe these various avenues to discover why a transition has not been made out of slow-reading phonics. Diagnosis should be pursued judiciously, causing the least possible emotional disturbance to the child, who will otherwise surely know what all the fuss is about.

## SUMMARY

Learning to read through a boost from no-rules phonics instruction will probably help the majority of kindergartners and first-graders. But such an aid must be viewed as a transitional phase in the process of learning to read with fluency and comprehension.

The use of decoding techniques in finding the sound equivalents of the letters and words the child encounters in her first reading books constitutes only a stage in a process that is not yet complete. To impose on the child a heavy system of rules with their many exceptions, thinking that this will lead to independence in decoding, can be extremely dangerous to the child. It will further slow up the child's pace of reading, leading to short-term memory "constipation" and the breakdown of comprehension. The basic goal of the reading process must always be finding meaning.

Instruction in phonics acquaints children with the sound equivalents of the print they are attempting to understand. At this point, children can take from their experience with spoken language the words and sentences that are familiar. The next step is processing these materials into deep-structured understanding.

The parent can thus understand that long-enduring decoding is a tedious process. It should never be the ultimate goal for the child's reading education. No matter how fast the child learns to decode written symbols into sound, the very process takes time, often leading to subvocalization, which is not a desirable end, either.

Therefore, be alert. Take all the commercial and ideological claims for phonics as the key to reading success with many grains of salt. Most of these claims are merely commercial exploitations. Be sensitive to the fact that, even as we have studied the process of reading acquisition for over a century, we—scholars, teachers, and parents—are still veritable neophytes. As we learn more, even what you have read above will be tempered by the new.

Now, onto the real mystery: the *reading system* and, then, successful quick and fluent reading with understanding and enjoyment.

## NOTE

1. S. Blumenfeld. 1973. *The New Illiterates*. New York: Arlington House. P. Copperman. 1980. *The Literary Hoax*. New York: Morrow-Quill.

# Chapter 5

# *The Child's Reading System*

## A GREAT EVENT

The maturation of the child's reading system makes it possible to leave phonics and slow reading and begin the rapid processing of words, sentences, and paragraphs into meaning. This can be done without the slow decoding of written words into their sound/spoken equivalents, and only then into meaning. This transition is a great but silent biological event in the developmental evolution of most children. It makes possible both the usefulness of written language and its limitless pleasures.

## STARTING TO READ

Since the days of the Sumerians, over 5,000 years ago, a tradition has grown up as to the prime moment when a child should begin to learn to read. This tradition has remained steady until recently, precisely because, more often than not, it worked. Now, especially in the United States, under political and other pressures for greater assurance of reading success, reading, especially in its readiness phases, is being introduced earlier and earlier. The reason for this is the now ever-more vulnerable child.

In the 1920s, research into this prime moment was undertaken in Chicago, a prime spot for scientific study. The conclusion of this research was that most children are ready to benefit from systematic reading instruction from about the age of six years and six months.

Here lay the tacit confirmation of this ancient tradition. In Europe for many centuries, and before in the ancient world of Rome, Greece, and beyond, instruction in reading normally commenced at age seven. This unspoken tradition can be understood as embodying the same logic as does the celebration of such religious solstice holidays as Christmas and Hanukkah, for example, which are usually held in the first few days after the turn of the sun.

So, too, age seven will capture many children who are not quite ready to read at age six-and-a-half. By age seven, almost every child ought to be ready to read. The child who is not ready will definitely receive special attention; the alarms ought to go off at that time for teachers as well as parents.

What do we mean by "ready"? This is the crux of this chapter's discussion. We certainly cannot mean ready in the perceptual/motor sense, since we have already discounted the significance of the supposed correlation between reading and the physical skills of balance, laterality coordination, figure recognition, and manipulation.

Some have proposed a correlation between intellectual maturity and readiness to read. Yet few children would be challenged intellectually by the stories that a six- or seven-year-old traditionally reads as part of first- or second-grade instruction. The stories are infantile in vocabulary and concept. Just listen, by contrast, to the ordinary conversation of children at this age, even to their street vocabulary.

Some within the profession today believe that there is no such thing as a "magic moment" when a child truly begins to read. The current view is that the entire process is an *emergent* one, wherein the child slowly develops all those skills that gradually are put in place in the child's psycho-neurological development, along with social and intellectual maturation. The theory is that ever so gradually, the child develops into a full reader.

In my opinion this view is in error. It has led to some extreme and dysfunctional pedagogical approaches to reading. It has also led to useless reading wars, both past and present, in which groups of partisans, armed with a partial truth, attempt to impose their half-truth on unknowing children, parents, teachers, and schools. It exemplifies our ongoing weakness for momentary educational nostrums.

Is the position proposed here just another panacea? I see the great historical tradition as partial support. Our own American tradition can be added to this. Consider the above-mentioned scientific research of the Chicago school in the 1920s, of William Gray and Carleton Washburne and their associates. For this research to have been adopted so universally as a developmental and pedagogical timing point, events had to have occurred in the life development of youngsters that were determining in the practices of parents and teachers, over a period of thousands of years of civilized and literate aspirations.

## THERE IS A MAGIC MOMENT

It should be understood that the phrase "magic moment" does not necessarily refer to a minute, hour, day, or even week. It is an event that is probably the product of the maturation of a set of unique neurological brain structures, associated with their visual and "linguistic" processing capacities.

Some medical researchers have hypothesized that such events are related to the myelination of the relevant nerve structures. Myelination is a process wherein a complex fatty acid—a protein film—is set down around the nerve connections. This helps to insulate the messages so that they don't short out on the way along the "wiring," to sputter about chaotically in random neurological space.

Scientific evidence points to concrete changes in the child's ability to graduate from decoding or mediated reading crutches to fluent or immediate reading. It is a discrete event in the development of the child's physical and mental maturity, not the gradual and almost infinitesimal emergence of a skill.

Quickly stated, this is a real developmental transition of which we, as parents and educators, must be aware so that we can better serve the child's literacy needs. What exactly happens in the child's reading behavior as a result of the magic moment?

First, the child is more quickly able to identify individual words. It is almost as if the child's phonics skill preparation and the consequent language sensitivity are internalized. Yet, as we will describe below, it is more than the look-say/sight word identification touted by the progressive educators of a generation ago.

Second, the child begins to be able to move visually and with comprehension through short sentences, and to do so ever more rapidly. We often become aware of this development through an occurrence as simple as a child's miscues, such as when the child substitutes her own words of similar meaning for the words actually on the printed page—"run" for "walk" or "Spot" for "Salt" [dog's name].

It is sometimes instructive to do no more than watch a child undergoing the process of silent reading, the tedious mouthing of sounds. Suddenly we may notice the smile of mental recognition, as the child reads an interesting or amusing passage. Parents and even teachers often describe this sharp learning transition as a miracle.

## CLUES TO A MYSTERY

If only the brightest of children were the first to learn to read, and seemingly with visual fluency and speed, the explanation of the difference between those young children who could and could not learn to read without slow phonics decoding would be simple.

Over the years, however, a large body of evidence, especially in the work of Delores Durkin, has accumulated to show that highly intelligent children, considering their chronological age, do not necessarily learn to read earlier or better than more average youngsters. The evidence has become persuasive through a wide variety of nonverbal testing procedures. Some of these tests are similar to the readiness tests given to kindergartners and preschoolers.

We should here include IQ tests, which when given to young children are still highly unreliable. These tests claim to invoke that enigmatic entity called "g" for general intelligence. Developmental factors, from the already familiar perceptual/motor development, to speech skills, have been found to be highly uncorrelated with the ability to learn to read fluently and early.

The awareness that "something else" was happening to children who read early was fueled by the research of Jane Torrey, an

African-American scholar who worked with very young minority children in Atlanta. Some of these children from poor and working-class families, without extraordinary intellectual, perceptual/motor, or speech skills, displayed uncanny visual abilities that allowed them to jump over the phonics phase of decoding by utilizing the kinds of clues given by television ads and programming.

In some manner, they were able to create an inner dictionary of shapes and forms that allowed them to transform the letters into words and meaning. Especially interesting was the great vernacular difference between the children's home speech and pronunciation and that of the television announcers and their ads. The children's minds seemingly disregarded the purely sound, or phonemic, differences, and went immediately to meaning or deep structure. It was enough to drive an advocate of the importance of phonics and the recognition of letter-to-sound relationships to extreme frustration.

Earlier experiments with so-called Kohler lenses may be instructive here. Kohler lenses act so as to turn our visual object world upside-down. After a certain amount of time, the brain acts to normalize ordinary perception, and even while the person continues to wear the lenses, the world turns itself right side up again. However, when directed toward written or other symbolic material, this normalization does not occur. The material stays turned upside down to the brain, mind, and perceptions. What does this mean?

One conclusion would be that not all perceptual experiences are interpreted by our brain in the same manner. Quite possibly, the parts of our brain that perceive and interpret objects are different in structure and location from those that perceive more abstract symbolic visual messages.

Such a conclusion also leads us to broader considerations about how children develop. We must propose that developmentally fluent reading is merely one among a series of independently maturing behavioral structures. Thus, a child might have marvelous vision, perhaps the perceptual/motor coordination of a Ted Williams—being able to see the almost discrete movements of a baseball as it approaches him and his bat at 100 miles per hour. At the same time, this same child might become a troubled reader.

The language/reading dimension of our perceptual and mental functioning is probably different from that which we use for seeing things. It is also semi-independent of our intellectual development, as are our phonics identification skills and our speaking abilities. We all have seen children who are enchanting talkers, yet, at the same time, are nonreaders.

Perhaps the most powerful piece of evidence arguing for the independent reality of the reading system in the development of the child's overall individuality arises from the now well-acknowledged fact that literally millions of youngsters and adults have clinically diagnosed reading disabilities.

*Dyslexia* is the generic term for such disabilities. We now know that so-called dyslexics have a wide variety of specific reading-function disabilities—reversing letters, inability to read in a straight pattern left to right, inability to distinguish differences in the shapes of letters, sometimes lack of a phonics sense of the differences in letters—in addition to other more traditional reading difficulties.

The importance of such reading disabilities is that they reveal to us the existence of a category of skills separate from the child's purely intellectual and other development pathways. Often these specific reading disabilities tend to disappear with age, the myelination and other developmental lags gradually coming into function at around age eight.

We do know that many individuals who are not seriously disabled by global reading and language dysfunctions (aphasia), can be retrained to find other modalities for learning—touch, for example—to access their deep-structured intelligence.

Here is the crux: The evidence indicates that a large proportion of the individuals who suffer in various degrees from *dyslexia* are persons of extremely high intelligence. This has been popularized in the literature to such an extent that a mythology has grown up—Thomas Edison, Albert Einstein, Winston Churchill, and, of course, the most famous and universal genius, Leonardo Da Vinci, a veritable who's-who of the smart and successful, are thought to have had learning disabilities of some kind.

At the other end of the spectrum are the so-called "word-callers." Although not too many of such children are found in ordinary heterogeneous classrooms today, teachers have been noting the existence of such children in their classrooms for several generations now. Because of our concern for first-grade reading success and the spread of reading readiness and other diagnostic early intervention programs, these children are mostly spotted early.

World-callers see the written word and translate it into its speech equivalent. They are often proficient oral readers, but they usually read in a monotone. Their voice inflection indicates no comprehension of what they read. When asked to answer questions about the meaning of a passage, whether they have read it silently or orally, they are unlikely to be able to do so. They have not been able to understand the meaning of what they have been able to decode phonetically.

There are increasing reports in the medical literature of research aimed toward identifying the relevant chromosomes from which this particular intellectual disability presumably derives. The disability is called *hyperlexia*. It shows up in children with early and seemingly virtuoso speech skills as well as the occasional child who can "read" on entering school.

From all these various clues, one can conclude that the reading system that allows the child to go beyond decoding to direct encoding to meaning—if all neurological systems are otherwise functioning properly—is a psycho-biological reality, and obviously varies in how it manifests itself in each child. The reading system, too, becomes an element in defining the unique individuality of each child, an element that is especially crucial, even poignant, as the child undergoes the tensions and comparisons that exist in any normal American classroom.

## THE READING SYSTEM AT WORK

At this point, it is fair to recognize the groundbreaking writings of Frank Smith on the relationship of the science of psycholinguistics to understanding reading. Smith's description of the crucial differences between mediated reading, phonic decoding, and immediate word and sentence recognition, that is, fluent reading, provides us with a crucial advance in our understanding.

Yet Smith did not admit to the reality of dyslexia. Also, he associated all fluent reading skills with the child's gradually advancing intellectual potentiality. He did not perceive the incongruity of a six-year-old's intellectual competencies and the infantile reading material on which she was being weaned. Because of this, he missed the realization that his excellent analysis of the process of fluent reading really described a discrete and crucial stage in the child's language development.

Smith, importantly, formulated the concept of *features* to explain how a child or an adult is able to read literally gobs of visual material, letters, words, sentences, even paragraphs, almost at a glance, 400–500 words a minute and more.

Smith postulated that as the fluent reader's eyes move along the horizontal line, left to right—in Chinese this would be vertically— the eyes at the same time move down the page diagonally, left to right. The fluent reader literally visually gulps large quantities of print, setting it immediately into mind as meaning and ideas.

Psycholinguists identify several associated movements in this process. This movement of the eye/mind takes place as a series of jumps, called *saccades*. In one second, the eye might make three or four such jumps; the landings down the page diagonally left to right are called *fixations*. Because it takes more time for the thinking mind to absorb these visual messages, the eye/mind usually goes backward in space to review the previous series of jumps and landings. This backward move is called a *regression*.

Features are the bits and pieces of visual information that the fluent reader uses when looking at the letters, words, sentences, and paragraphs. This concept is what I have previously called a visual/perceptual dictionary. It translates the relevant differences between letters and words into an almost automatic recognition system by which the reader goes beyond the older sight/sound system. The featural system is geared to provide meaning from these visual bits of information: letter similarities/differences; word similarities/differences; crucial sentence similarities/differences.

It is not known yet how this happens or where in the brain the process of featural encoding takes place. It is probable that for every human being, slightly different features are recognized, others ignored, so as to help the individual see these patterns and thus recognize enough visual material for comprehension to take place. It is important that the person should never actually have to see too much of the letters and words and so to overload short-term memory.

The term *features* is thus used to describe the fact that good readers never actually look at the total visual image of the letter, word, sentence, or, obviously, the total paragraph. They see enough in the bits and pieces of visual information on the page to get as much meaning as they need. One of the interesting elements in the understanding of fluent reading is that the intellectual part of the brain is also at work guiding the automatic element of the reading/featural system to decide how detailed a visual/meaning structure needs to be obtained.

Certainly, one learns to read a newspaper or novel differently than one reads a technical computer manual. And it would be most inefficient were one to read a modern romance novel at the same pace and intensity as one would read the existential writings of Karl Jaspers. These kinds of reading decisions—how carefully, rapidly, slowly, whether even simply to skim—arise from a series of intellectual considerations that one makes. The child should be taught early to self-monitor such decisions.

The understanding of the idea of features in the process of learning to read words and sentences rapidly has allowed us to place in perspective the old look-say pedagogy of beginning reading. We now understand that while the child may seem to be identifying words and short sentences, she is actually creating her internal featural dictionary of differences in shapes and contexts out of which meaning is created. In the long run, the dictionary will go beyond the letters and words that first concerned her, to sentences and paragraphs as entire meaning units.

## THE INITIAL TEACHING ALPHABET

One final clue about features may help the parent, teacher, even young reader better understand this mysterious process. The clue is ITA, the Initial Teaching Alphabet (see Tables 5.1 and 5.2). ITA was invented by Sir James Pitman, whose grandfather, it is interesting to note, created the Pitman shorthand system. The Initial Teaching Alphabet was intended to mimic the forty-four phonemes of spoken English. The idea was that a five-year-old child could learn the sound equivalents of the forty-four graphemes or letters that stood for each sound in our language.

Our twenty-six-letter alphabet, as discussed in Chapter 4, has so many exceptions-to-the-rule that Pitman saw the regularity of these forty-four "created" letters, most of them identical to the traditional orthography (letters), as a distinct learning advantage for the beginning reader. Children could also learn to write by sounding out the material, without any of the above special situations and exceptions with which they normally have to deal in traditional orthography (TO), or letters.

**Table 5.1**
**The Initial Teaching Alphabet (ITA)**

æ   b   c   d   ⴹ
face   bed   cat   dog   key

f   g   h   ⱨ   j   k
feet   leg   hat   fly   jug   key

l   m   n   œ   p
letter   man   nest   over   pen

r   s   t   ⱳ   v   w
red   spoon   tree   use   voice   window

y   z   ʒ   wh   ch
yes   zebra   daisy   when   chair

th   ᵼh   ʃh   ʒ   ŋ
three   the   shop   television   drink

ɑ   au   a   e   i   o
father   ball   cap   egg   milk   box

u   ω   ⍵   ou   oi
up   book   spoon   out   oil

## ʃhe littl red hen

ωuns upon a tiem littl red hen livd
in a barn wiʃh her fiev chicks. a pig,
a cat and a duck mæd ʃhær hœm in
ʃhe sæm barn. ⴹⴹch dæ littl red hen
led her chicks out tω lωk for fωd
but ʃhe pig, ʃhe cat and ʃhe duck
wωd not lωk for fωd.

Logic supports the many efforts to reform the way we spell, but it becomes less practical every year as the amount of printed material increases using the established patterns.
The impact of the child's environment invalidates efforts to control experimentation with
new alphabets.

**Table 5.2**
**Phonics-Consistent Beginning Reading**

everyþiŋ woɾ reḑy. it woɾ tiem
for tæk-off but ʃhe skie woɾ still not
cleer.

ſam ʃhe spæsman woɾ saḑ. "ɨe hav
wæteḑ and wæteḑ for ʃhis big ḑæ," heɛ
seḑ tɷ himself. "ŋou ɨe mæ hav tɷ wæt
still loŋgeɾ tɷ flɨe mɨe spæs ʃhip
arɷnd ʃhe erþh."

Everything was ready. It was time
for take-off but the sky was still not
clear.

Sam the spaceman was sad. "I have
waited and waited for this big day," he
said to himself. "Now I may have to wait
still longer to fly my space ship
around the earth."

Many children easily learned to read using the ITA because of its phonemic regularity. The extra letters or graphemes did not seem to interfere with the learning process, even for kindergartners. What was quite exciting about ITA was that when the young ITA users' reading systems matured (Pitman and his followers did not understand this concept then and therefore did not explain it as we do), the children were able to make the transfer from ITA to TO without any difficulty. Why?

The answer is that the upper parts of even the new graphemes—the ITA letter symbols—corresponded exactly to their closest-sounding letters in TO. The child who was making the transition to fluent reading was looking at the upper parts of the letters and words to obtain the relevant featural (shape) information from which to make the meaning inferences.

## THE READING SYSTEM: A DEVELOPMENTAL REALITY

Historically, though with some exceptions, literacy was attained only by a minority of the people of the great civilizations. A social skill which over 5000 years of civilizational development was never accomplished by the vast majority of the populace should, unlike speech, be seen as an individually variable skill. We therefore should not be surprised that not all children will develop equal reading skills, even assuming equal intellectual capabilities. It is important for parents and teachers to be sensitive to the variability in the onset of that magic moment when and how fluent reading comes into play.

Some children will never be good readers. They will display other talents, and should be encouraged to develop intellectually and emphasize the skills that can further these talents. They could be engineers, scientists, architects, or artists, have political, musical, or mathematical abilities, none of which are fatally undercut by weak reading skills, even dyslexia.

One issue remains to be noted here. It will be developed in the next chapter. This is the relationship between the automatic characteristics of the featural reading system and the individual's deeper, more general, intellectual capabilities. Often we see a child who seems to have the minimum word and sentence identification skills that are encompassed in the featural/fluent reading system.

Yet this child moves ever so slowly through the beginning readers and then the early elementary grade basals and accompanying reading material.

It is possible, though the research is inconclusive as yet, that weak intelligence, though not at the retardation level, is accompanied by only moderate featural reading skills. There is no sharp line that divides those children who are in general slow to learn (yet with fairly well-developed abilities to read fluently) and those with the absolute retardation levels of the *hyperlexic*.

Next, we must look into the role that human intelligence plays in its interaction with the reading system of skills. Intelligence is a delicate issue to discuss, either with or among parents and teachers. However, the core of reading ability is meaning or comprehension. And we do recognize the central role of such language competencies for the evolution of civilization.

In fact, tests of verbal reading and writing skills have proved to be the most predictive instrument that are presently available when we want to estimate both the educational and the vocational future of an individual. Central to all such testing goals is understanding. The ultimate criterion of reading success is the ability to see relationships, to make distinctions, and to determine what does or does not belong in a category of things or ideas.

In sum, the intellectual manipulation of written and symbolic information can be achieved only through skilled reading.

# Chapter 6

## *Reading Is Understanding*

### INTELLIGENCE ENTERS THE EQUATION

Third grade has been found to be the beginning of the great divide. By the end of third grade, the developmental differences between children's reading systems have usually evened out. By this time, the decoders, the slow myelinators, the immature students, all have achieved a relative state of neurological maturity regarding their preparedness for reading comprehension.

I leave aside those who have been destroyed by systematic phonics instruction. But I do include the many who have always suffered from what is, at the least, "benign" educational neglect. They have not had much in the way of daily reading and general language instruction. So much can be accomplished if the mind is interested, for the mere association with a print-laden environment, at home or in the classroom, can show the child the way.

It is probably true that children who have been the victims of instructional neglect can catch up by grade three, if there are books around and the other children in class are reading. This form of spontaneous absorption of reading skills has been adopted for centuries by ordinary people interested in knowing what is going on in the world. Of course, books and other reading material have to be available. Also, someone must be there to offer a few clues as to how the reading process works.

The third-grade Rubicon, as attested to by many studies, shows that the differences between the best and the poorest readers begin to increase sharply. This is now reflected in IQ and achievement testing in subject matter areas as well as in ordinary reading and writing. Children at this level are now getting closer to their intellectual levels as skill in reading more rapidly increases.

This should be a warning to parents and teachers to go slowly in drawing any conclusions about a particular child's long-term reading prospects before the middle of third grade. Of course, this caution excludes those children who clearly display a reading system disability, possible dyslexia, or children who seem "slow" in all that they do, in school and out. Such children will display poor spoken vocabulary, lack of interest in the learning material, and lethargy both in the classroom and at home when it comes to mental matters. At the same time, these children could be physically quite active and aggressive.

The bright child, with all her reading systems "go"—this includes the ability to write—will begin to move rapidly forward as her comprehension takes her mind through larger and ever more advanced quantities of reading material. Occasionally this child will be weaker, perhaps in mathematics, or in another subject matter. The mind does not always move homogeneously over the entire range of subject matters with either interest or success.

What we call intelligence is a mysterious thing, and we should try to take into account its still unclear nature. It manifests itself differently in each child. The brightest children may not all be top-notch readers or number crunchers.

## TWO SYSTEMS WORKING TOGETHER

It is important that we discuss here the relationship between the gradually maturing reading system of the child as she moves through the early grades and her evolving intelligence—immature, yes, but still an important indicator at this prepubescent age level. Despite our continuing ignorance of the operation of these mental functions, we know of their existence and variable expression in different individuals. Effective education of our children depends on using what we understand to be real.

We should not avoid the fact that we still have much to learn. Such denial only leads to an eternal and inchoate groping that undercuts our desires to help those in need. On the other hand, we have to treat this knowledge and/or ignorance delicately and carefully. Let us not ever be too sure of ourselves. Approach every educational and behavioral suggestion and program with a sense of: "Be careful, we could be wrong and do wrong."

Let us return to the reading system. Some four- and five-year-olds are into full-scale featural reading. They are *reading* words, not just decoding them to sound. Often they are able to put together short sentences into meaning, recognition, and smiling achievement.

On the other hand, many youngsters at seven, eight, or even nine year of age, although not clinically dyslexic, have difficulty putting together the visual features of words into meaningful wholes. Some of these children may be slow intellectually—this may be developmental slowness or possibly an indication of permanently low intelligence. The parent and teacher should remember that one of the reasons one child will score so variably on tests given at different age levels, even taking into account the health and emotional states of the child when she is tested, is that children have widely different developmental chronologies. They speed up and they slow down. This all calls for evaluative caution.

The two systems of reading begin to function as children's reading systems can increasingly integrate the visual marks with speed and fluency, invoking the powers of their intelligence to move through the page for comprehension. It is important to understand that the reading system is on "automatic." With some children, it begins to function spontaneously—the magic moment—usually before age seven.

It is the child's deeper and more voluntarily invoked powers of thought that will stimulate the eyes and the neurology of the reading system to move rapidly over the written material. Therefore, it is important that children be taught to move their eyes quickly ahead of what they are reading, both silently and orally.

Speed Reading teacher Evelyn Wood starts the process of helping her students increase their reading speed by suggesting that they cover the material immediately below what they are reading with a piece of cardboard, moving it down the page so as to reveal the written material at an ever more rapid speed. In a sense we are training the eye not to be lazy, for a good mind and an intact reading system can "gulp" much more information from the features on the page than we normally expect.

An example of how the mind works through the reading system to beckon it quickly forward into comprehension can be seen in the following psycholinguistic explanation of the choices that our minds must make in reading a single sentence. The sentence is interrupted by a page turn in which the last letters of the last word are omitted: "The bus was parked in its ga-" [page turn].

What strategies can the child use to figure out what completes the sentence? (1) She may turn the page—a purely visual physical solution. (2) She may guess the letter possibilities vis-à-vis her experience with letter combinations—the next syllable will probably begin with a consonant. If the child guesses that the next letter is o as in "gaol," knows that "gaol" means a British "jail," and is younger than fourteen, make way for her. (3) If the child uses the regularities of English syntax and proposes a word such as "garden" or "gas station," that is, a noun rather than a verb or adverb such as "gallop" or "galore," it indicates sensitivity to grammatical regularities or usage. Finally (4), the most probable semantic or meaningful answer would be ga*rage*. The guesses "garden" or even "gas station" would tell us something interesting about the child's understanding or creativity.

A teacher or parent could devise exercises such as these to test children's various skills at mastering the ambiguities of written language. At the least, the above example sensitizes us to the many spontaneous, logical decisions that have to be made by our minds in the early stages of reading maturity.

Readers in reality make such guesses or assumptions momentarily and constantly as they whiz along and down the page at several hundred words a minute, hoping that their guesses within the page make sense. For they are only looking at bits and pieces of words, sentences, and paragraphs as these enter the eye/mind for understanding.

## PREDICTING AND RELATING

The eyes move rapidly in fluent reading. But the mind moves ever farther ahead of the eyes to find out what is being "said" in the print. What is happening inside the minds of these curious new readers? Two concepts, not mutually exclusive, for understanding what we are doing when we comprehend written material at a quick and fluent rate are *predicting* and *relating*.

### Predicting

Predicting is used by Frank Smith to explain how an individual determines the meaning of what is on the page from essentially small amounts of visual materials—the bits and pieces. These bits and pieces are rapidly extracted from a much larger quantity of actual print—the many letters in the paragraphs being read.

Children, according to the concept of prediction, are constantly making guesses as to what comes next. They use the various visual, grammatical, and semantic language clues discussed above. If they discover that their guess is wrong, they will have to self-correct and internalize the "why" of their mistake. This will help them avoid the error the next time similar word/idea combinations occur. In this way, the rhythmic pleasures and free flow of understanding that children derive from fast reading will not be hindered.

Prediction has a somewhat linear cast. One wonders if the child is in any meaningful sense putting out a directional series of "questions"—what's next?—as she reads through a page of fiction. A word that better describes what children or adults do when they read might be expecting.

### Relating

The reason for saying that the mind goes out "in front of the child's eyes" is that any phonetic or spelling irregularities of our language require quick, almost instantaneous interpretations or reinterpretations of the visual print material. Also, as oral and silent readers can tell us (musicians reading music, also), since there is a mental/perceptual lag, if the mind does *not* constantly move ahead of the written material, comprehension will be retarded. Thinking and access to deep structure take time. That is why tall musical instrumentalists and tall basketball players have problems if their eyes and minds are not out ahead of their body reactions: thought messages take time to traverse the neurological space between receptor intake and mental and physical organization and action.

Perhaps the word *"relating"* better conveys what children are doing when they are reading for comprehension. For in understanding what one is reading, a person does not receive back from the print a series of "confirm" or "disconfirm" messages. Rather, the mind searches to fit the new information into that rich, three-dimensional web of meaning, both in space and time, that makes up every human being's singular map of experience. The term *relating* helps us to envision the connections between the new information and the old. This search for meaning, of course, applies as well to fictional stories as it does to social studies or science reading.

The dynamics of the comprehension process that integrates the two systems, the featural and meaning systems, requires us to view the comprehension system as leaping out ahead of the reading system. The reading system, whose "point men" are the eyes, will

**Figure 6.1**
**Model of Slow and Fast Reading**

---

**Slow Reading, or the Phonic Model**

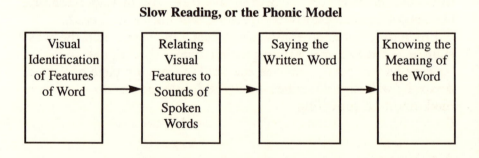

**Fast Fluent Reading for Meaning**

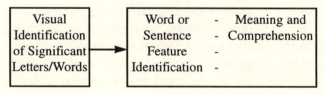

receive the primary featural messages, thence transmitting them back into the integrating neurology of the featural system and, finally, deep into the cortex, where the relationships are organized. Then comes the confirming smile of "aha" on the youngster's face—understanding.

## EDUCATIONAL PATHWAYS

An important principle to remember in the literacy education of our children is that understanding and knowledge lie deep and inchoate in our brains. As far as we know, no neat little rows and lists of knowledge line up for us to push-button into virtual reality when we speak and write.

We must access this knowledge and construct into external form through the symbols of knowledge, mathematics, music, writing, and, of course, speech. All of us have felt at one time or another that we understood something—that we had it in our minds. At the same time, we must be able to express it in clear, logical sequences of words, sentences, and paragraphs. In other words, until we put our ideas into these observable forms, we do not really have knowledge.

This is why, when children read silently in their classrooms, as they should most often after first grade, instead of slow oral reading, it is the obligation of teachers and parents to expect the children to answer questions or explain in their own words what they have read, or write down a summary.

It is all down there, deeply lodged in the chemistry of our cortical neurology. We cannot function effectively in society if we do not have enough knowledge interrelated in this web. But if we are untrained in the language areas to access and use this knowledge, we are likewise destined to be frustrated and ineffectual humans. And, of course, to get the knowledge into our brains, we ideally would have had richly informational experiences, including listening and understanding as well as the technical skill of being able to read efficiently.

Thus, the educational imperative in the elementary grades and beyond is to immerse children in a wide and interesting variety of language experiences that use the four modalities of language—listening, speaking, reading, and writing. The point of every moment of immersion should always be the gaining of meaning—what kind of language/conceptual skill is the child achieving at this point? The necessity for close parent-teacher participation is critical, because only a more experienced guide can pattern these skill exercises in a developmental sequence, constantly challenging the child to reach further.

What are some ideas? Writing reports based on book research, playing map games, doing vocabulary expansion games, learning new words, and writing them in sentences, hunting out interesting words in new books, creating a child's dictionary of new words, and incorporating them in creative writing, speaking the new words and ideas in presentations to classmates (or to brothers, sisters, or parents). New computer programs, together with printers, now allow even very young children to learn to spell new and sometimes esoteric words, then to have them printed out as labels, to be worn proudly.

Vocabulary is an important aspect of language fluency because words take on meaning by virtue of their relationship with the meanings of other words. In fact, some psychometricians (testers of intelligence) believe that vocabulary competency is the most accurate and predictive quick test of intelligence potentiality. Being able to describe quickly the meaning of a paragraph; being challenged to answer complex questions about historical, scientific, geographical passages; even being able to use bus and train schedules competently, are likewise grist for future literacy.

In our pedagogical approach to the child, we must be constantly "bouncing" the child's present ability to figure things out linguistically off the boundaries of the possible, to try ever more complex problems. Never assume that a child is too young, immature, or slow to try the next step. If the child is not yet ready, go back.

This is why reading teachers have always had a triarchic view of the reading process: (1) the lowest or independent level, at which the child is sure to be able to read for understanding and pleasure on her own; (2) the instructional level, where new and/or challenging material is dealt with under the careful eye of the teacher or parent; and (3) the so-called frustration level, where children are challenged to try out material as difficult as they can be reasonably expected to understand, and then to analyze the extent of their problems in dealing with it, or their learning frustrations and discouragement. Sometimes we learn more about a child's skills and needs from such "frustration" pedagogy than from traditional strategies.

## THE BREADTH OF LANGUAGE

"She speaks much, but says nothing." A truism, indeed, but it sends an important message. We must always make a distinction between the so-called surface-structure skills of people, all of our children, and the deep-structure competencies that surface-structure behaviors often mask. Some people are fluent fulminators. Others are bumbling brilliants.

Graduate student gossip at Columbia University underlines a relevant tale. In the Department of Classics were two famous figures. One, a Latinist, wrote many books on language and literature, and had a nationally syndicated radio program in which he discussed current cultural issues and writings. The other, a scholar of classical Greek, was not nearly as well known. His reputation as an almost incoherent lecturer brought smiles around the campus.

However, this scholar of Greek drew a disproportionate number of graduate students to him for their doctoral research. The Latinist was relatively ignored despite his fame and fluency. The word from students in that department was that the Latinist had little to say, whereas the Greek scholar "sputtered" with great depth and wisdom.

This illustrates why teachers and parents must be on the watch, remembering that language skills, while always important, are intermediary vehicles for a mind's potentiality—for a mind often struggling to break loose from deep structure to the surface. The important thing is that the individual needs to acquire enough skills to be able to express her potential.

Spelling, a surface-structure skill, can now be assisted by computer spell check programs. But try devising a computer program that will assist the individual in writing a term paper that shows depth of research and understanding!

Language is the great broad river of human intellectual expression. An individual with a powerful mind needs sufficient language skills to probe a great variety of disciplines. An individual needs enough language facility to unlock such disciplines as computing, music, mathematics, architecture, management, and engineering, all areas that involve the manipulation of symbol systems derived from the linguistic base.

For contemporary examples; today, a number of developing nations in the far East—such as China, Malaysia, and Thailand—

have undereducated work forces as compared to Europe. Workers from these nations often have as little as a fourth-grade education. Yet it has been found that they can be educated on the job to equal the competency levels of the Europeans.

This situation seems to mirror what occurred in Japan in the post–World War II period, when modestly educated workers were able to make the quick and constant changes necessary to retrain themselves for higher and more complex tasks well beyond their formal educational backgrounds.

Reeducation on the job might be the theme of these events. Building on a modest formal base of educational skills, quite high levels of vocational/technological performance seem to be created. Indeed, in the early nineteenth century, the same situation occurred in the United States, when modestly literate farm children were retrained through the factory/dormitory system.

Experience is once more telling us that in certain settings a limited literacy foundation can become the lever for an individual's subsequent learning/skill increments. If these workers in developing nations have, at a minimum, fourth-grade reading and writing skills, then surely it is a world-class fourth-grade level, not necessarily comparable to the fourth-grade level of schools in the United States.

Another example can be found in the SAT scores that college-bound students achieve in order to find the institution appropriate to their skills and interests. It is rare to find a high school junior or senior with extremely high math scores, 650–800 (range 200–800) who at the same time has extremely low scores on the verbal section. On the other hand, we find many high scorers on the verbal tests who score extremely poorly in the math area. (This is especially true among females.)

Researchers still see the SAT verbal score as the most predictive score in these same higher ranges, 650–800. This is because, in contrast to how they can prepare for the verbal test, students can more readily study for the math SAT as a skill area. Naturally, when we view the highest level of math achievement, where purely abstract abilities show themselves, we are probably witnessing the flowering of great mental powers.

But because the classic verbal SAT dipped into such a breadth of human experience, into so many diverse intellectual surface- and deep-structure skills, it still served as the more predictive of the two areas for long-term educational potentiality.

**Table 6.1**
**Differences Between Good Readers and Poor Readers**

| GOOD READERS | POOR READERS |
|---|---|
| **Before Reading** | |
| Build up their background knowledge on the subject. | Start reading without thinking about the subject. |
| Know their purpose for reading. | Do not know why they are reading. |
| Focus their complete attention on reading. | |
| **During Reading** | |
| Give their complete attention to the reading task. | Do not know whether they understand or do not understand. |
| Keep a constant check on their own understanding. | Do not monitor their own comprehension. |
| Monitor their reading comprehension and do it so often that it becomes automatic. | Seldom use any of the fix-up strategies. |
| Stop only to use a fix-up strategy when they do not understand. | |
| **After Reading** | |
| Decide if they have achieved their goal for reading. | Do not know what they have read. |
| Evaluate comprehension of what was read. | Do not follow reading with comprehension self-check. |
| Summarize the major ideas in a graphic organizer. | |
| Seek additional information from outside sources. | |

Poor readers often improve radically when
they are explicitly taught the above rules.

These facts require of educators, including parents and teachers, steady attention to the language and reading development of the child. On the other hand, after a systematic effort to build skills and knowledge, the student may be only modestly talented in these essentially surface-structure skills. Then it is incumbent on us to probe deeper, to see if we can find other abilities that might shine through, despite the student's limited facility in the language area.

Ultimately that is the point of education: to draw out what is deeply embedded as potentiality in children, and to find the means for this power to be usefully expressed. The beneficiaries will be the world around them as well as the children themselves.

# Chapter 7

# First Grade Rubicon: Ten Important Tips

1. Build up a sight vocabulary of words that the child can recognize by shape and sound, particularly shape. Gradually increase the number of words that the child is challenged to recognize in stories, of ever greater complexity, but slowly and with care to accommodate her pace of recognition.

2. For the early stages of first grade, utilize whatever mediated reading phonics aids seem necessary to help children recognize words as visual entities that have meaning. By now, children should know the names and sounds of the letters in relation to the words they speak.

Differences in words, such as those between "trip" and "trap," should be recognized early on. Skills in seeing and hearing differences in words—"tip" and "sip," "plum" and "pluck," "sap" and "sat," "heat" and "eat"—are important way stations on the road toward awareness of the different features, or shapes of words that look almost alike, sometimes even sound alike, but have important meaning differences.

Remember that these perceptions of similarity and difference in words should *not* be accompanied by the learning of phonics rules. The child will gradually internalize these principles as a dictionary of sight differences in words that have their own unique meanings.

3. Motivation at this stage in the reading game is crucial. After all, these are five-, six-, and seven-year-olds. We need to make them comfortable with reading and we want to stimulate them to learn. They must want to learn to identify ever more new words in the context of enjoyable stories. Parents and teachers must walk a delicate line between providing praise for correct guesses and identifications, while also offering miscue corrections (correct meaning but wrong word), and phonetic assistance with decoding difficult words that the child knows only from speech.

The goal is success, however the teacher or parent can accomplish it. If the child seems to have problems, it is best to slow down the instruction, and search for the problem through a systematic diagnosis. *We don't want the child to turn off.*

4. If there is success in the sight word recognition process, occasionally challenge the child to the point of frustration, but delicately. We always want to know what the child can be stimulated to achieve. Therefore, we must search for the upper range of accomplishment in word and sentence recognition, comprehension of stories and their interpretation, as well as the written and number skills learning that accompanies the learning-to-read drama.

5. Favor oral reading at this stage in the instructional process. It is slow enough so that the child can balance speech and comprehension. Expression in oral reading will often clue in the listener to the level of understanding of the material attained by the reader.

Discourage children from pointing to the words while they are reading. Such pointing can often slow down the reading process and thus undermine comprehension. Slow reading often causes the child to forget the drift of a sentence before she finishes it.

It is important, even in oral reading, to ask children questions about a story they have just finished reading. Do this both with the book open—so that children can look back at the story they have just read—and also with the book closed—to see how much of the story has penetrated their understanding. Occasionally, especially in "fun" oral reading, ask questions during the story to check attention to comprehension and reinforcement of the idea of reading.

6. Reading a story with a simple line of meaning and pictures to help with the context is a good way to begin reading instruction for sight recognition of words. Often, however, bright children begin to get lazy and guess the words that they are supposed to be reading. They can fool many a teacher and parent, who finally catch on when the child makes too many miscues, guessing the correct meaning but not the right words on the page.

How can we guarantee that children truly have a sight vocabulary that they can quickly identify, either by sight or through rapid decoding to sound? One way is to ask them occasionally to read words apart from a story that they have previously read and learned. It is even useful simply to have children read words from a list, and, to learn the meaning of the relevant nouns and verbs. Perhaps they can orally create a sentence from one or more words that they have read from the list. Any one of such methods will show us whether a child is progressing in word recognition and comprehension.

7. Good first-grade language activities include word analysis, breaking up compound words (playland, motorcycle, or campground), recognizing the different forms of the plural (_____s, _____es, etc.), and using a group of words on a black or felt board to create different simple sentences and putting them together in new ways. These are all useful skill-building activities.

However, such activities should not engage too much of children's time. They should always and overwhelmingly be absorbed in actual reading activity. Many of these skills are silently absorbed by children in the context of reading. It is best to find out if children understand these principles from the actual reading of stories or factual material. "Do you know what the 's' at the end of 'dragons' means?" or "What about the words 'motorboat' and 'motorcycle?'" What is similar in each word and what is different, and what do they mean?

8. On occasion, children should be asked to sight-read a simple story that the parent or teacher feels to be well within their reading level. This affords a good opportunity to find out the state of children's independence and self-monitoring abilities.

Also, a break from the controlled vocabulary of the basal reader or learning series of books is always refreshing. It offers the opportunity for the child to realize her accomplishments by reading a genuine work of literature and can certainly be a gratifying and morale-boosting occasion.

If such sight-reading is successful, it can offer the parent and teacher the opportunity to wean the child from reliance on the basal readers. Also, it may be the time to strike out into the uncharted waters of new vocabulary challenges as well as complex grammatical constructions of meaning. Some children will flower under such a teaching regime. Others will flounder. Be careful.

9. Remember the goal: Your child should be guided toward recognizing words, and then short sentences, as visual/meaning units. See phonics and sounding out words as only temporary crutches. We help the child in mediated or slow reading so that she can achieve the visual recognition of a word, even after decoding it to sound and comparing it to the spoken version.

Eventually we want the child to see the words and the sentences that are formed from words as visual wholes without the slowing up that decoding and sounding-out force upon the child. True reading will occur only when the child's reading system matures to the point that she can rapidly encode the features of the words that her eyes pass over on the page. Help the child by accentuating the visual recognition of words as the important goal of the reading process.

10. Be aware of the danger signals: It is June of first grade. The child in question turned seven years old this past December 27. One or more of the following situations has occurred by early June. They are listed in order of increasing seriousness.

a. The child has some decoding abilities. She can get most beginning sounds, often guessing the final and middle phonemes of the word. But she doesn't read words, she mostly has good guesses.

b. It is all chaos, with random success both in reading words and understanding the relationship between seeing simple consonants, vowels, their combinations, and the relationship of print to the spoken language. Number skills are average, but writing is a disaster, with scribbles and reversals of shape and order of simple words such as "dog," "hat."

c. The child can sound out words with seeming consistency. She even has a small sight vocabulary that does not first require decoding to sound. Thus, her oral reading is not at the bottom of the class. Writing her letters and simple words shows a clarity of penmanship and control. Simple number concepts, however, are rudimentary. Most frightening is her oral reading, which is in a monotone, indicating a lack of understanding of the story line.

There is only slight comprehension of simple nouns and verbs, such as "cat," "mommy," "run."

Don't panic. Often, chaotic first-grade programs, where the teacher does not meet the child's needs for gradual but systematic teaching, will leave first graders swimming around in confusion. But if the parents have been following the progress of their child throughout the year, conferring with the teacher, and themselves working with the child at home, and have been noticing that these symptoms are not related to the classroom teaching approach, it is time for restrained action.

The child should start working with a reading specialist for more careful diagnostic analysis. Summer lies ahead. If the parents are wise and themselves disciplined for gentle and careful one-on-one work with their child, applying the advice of teacher and reading specialist, second grade might yet be a success for the child.

# Chapter 8

# *Each Child Is Unique*

## POINT OF VIEW

In order to learn to read, every child must pass through the same developmental transitions. The completion of these transitions will result in a mesh of communication and understanding between the writer and the reader. In the average elementary classroom, children who have attained at least the early stages of fluency will themselves share in this understanding.

The problem is that there is no average child. They are all *sui generis*, that is, unique unto themselves. And they often vary from the norm in ways that significantly affect their general learning and reading progress. Taking into account knowledge that has been set forth in the previous chapters concerning the process of learning to read by the "average" child, it might be useful to use this knowledge to examine those children who differ significantly from the norm in their special reading circumstances.

What follows is a series of short essays that will attempt to lay down general parameters for dealing with these special reading situations. The intent is to communicate both to parents and teachers how to best approach each situation in question. From a long-distance standpoint, one can never diagnose and propose in specifics. However, I believe that it is helpful to be alert, so that you can be ready to intervene with the proper concrete parental and teacher educational responses.

## EARLY READERS

Sarah and Seth represent two types of early readers that teachers often encounter in preschool programs. Not all children come to early reading in the same way. They, thus represent interesting and still mysterious dimensions to the development of reading ability in young children.

### Sarah

Sarah is the more typical early reader, perhaps only because her achievements as a precocious four-year-old fit into what we expect will develop as she reaches first grade and beyond. Sarah is an early fluent reader.

What is interesting about Sarah is that one would not ordinarily expect such an ability coming from a child of her background. Sarah is the middle daughter in a family of five children; her parents are typical blue-collar, working-class folks. Her father is a trucker; her mother holds the family together in their small three-bedroom ranch, as Dad is away on his long-haul routes for most of the week.

To her teachers in the community preschool she attends, Sarah's ability to put together words from the letters and illustrations that describe these letters—"t" for "tiger," "d" for "duck," for example— with only the barest and most casual hints about the sounds of the letters to guide her, were no less than astounding.

Naturally, the teachers in the school, being sensitive to the unique needs of the different children in the class, even for the few hours in the morning that the children were in class, jumped at the opportunity to work with Sarah on the preprimers. These she virtually gobbled up, reading words and then simple sentences with ease, with rarely a move of the lips.

**Table 8.1**
**A Reader at Age Three**

---

Mother had read to April from the time she was one year old. At age 3 years 4 months, April was visited by a professor (P.), who asked April to read *Ducky's Mother*, a story that had been read to her many times. April read in an enthusiastic manner and with good intonation. She read the entire book, portions of which follow:

| April | Story |
|---|---|
| Out popped the little ducky. | Out came the little duck. |
| Ducky said, "Where is my mother?" (Aside, to P., Ducky's looking for it.) | "Where is my mother?" Ducky said. He looked for her. |
| Looked up, didn't see her. | Ducky looked up. He did not see her. |
| And he looked down. He didn't see it. | Ducky looked down. He did not see her. |
| So Ducky said he's going to look for mommy. | "I will go and look for her," Ducky said. |
| * * * * * * * | * * * * * * * |
| Came to a puppy and he said, "Are you my mother?" | He came to a puppy. "Are You my mother?" Ducky said to the puppy. |
| "Mmm. . ." He didn't say anything. Puppy just looked and looked. | The puppy just looked and looked. He did not say a thing to Ducky. |
| Ducky came to a big goose and he said, "You look like my mother." "No." | The puppy was not his mother, so he walked on. Then he came to a big goose. "Are you my mother?" Ducky said to the big goose. "No," said the goose. |

---

Sarah was a talker and a social busybody in her sweet, four-year-old way. She was somewhat bossy in her relations with the other children, her diminutive stature not interfering at all with her self-concept and her view of the power that exists in the world out there. By the time Sarah completed her year with the other four-year-olds in June, she was reading first-grade reading materials, simple stories, and nonfiction.

To her teachers, she seemed bright but not extremely aware of the events of the world outside, nor was she interested in the world of knowledge in a way that might lead them to consider her a candidate for prodigy status. Simple testing with readiness tests, however, placed her in the above-average range.

What seemed to stand out was her ability to go directly from the print matter to understanding words and sentences, and to do this with speed and fluency. In fact, it was surprising that her oral reading was, by the middle of the year, slower than her silent reading skills. The latter was always tested out by the teachers and found to be "on-the-mark" as to comprehension.

All in all, Sarah represented a classic early fluent reader. In some manner, this child's neurology had developed far more rapidly than one would have expected. Her personality and self-esteem were likewise beyond her years. Yet, on balance, Sarah was a child none of the teachers felt (and assented to by her parent, who had already experienced the growing pains of four other children) showed extreme intellectual brilliance, at least as yet. She was a good reader, and she enjoyed every moment of her special gift.

## Seth

Seth is a more unusual type of early reader. One doesn't discover the talents of children like Seth in the typical preschool. This is because he has turned out to be a precocious decoder. The reason for the rarity in the display of his abilities is that decoding is usually taught as part of the reading program, most often begun in a regular way in first grade.

It is only when very young children are subject to systematic reading instruction that we sometimes learn of such gifts. Seth's father is a pediatrician, his mother a grade school teacher. The family is upper middle class and attentive to the educational progress of their two children. Seth has a brother three years older than he, who was also given intensive reading instruction by their mother, starting at about age three-and-a-half.

Seth's brother made only limited reading progress. Mother, a wise educator, held off, allowing him to progress in reading with his peers. He became fluent early in first grade, just beyond his sixth birthday. Seth was started on the same regimen when he was close to four years old. Mother showed Seth the letters, their sounds, and their visual equivalents—"b" for "baby," "c" for "cat."

At first, Seth would forget the visual names of the letters. But, differently from his brother, Seth spoke the words clearly when asked to repeat them by Mother. He also seemed to remember the sounds more easily than the names. By the time the teachers in the progressive preschool that Seth attended began to present to the children the letters of the alphabet and their sound equivalents (this in the four-year-old group the following fall), Seth was already able to sound out many words, and his visual retention of the images was good enough to trigger a real skill in relating sounds of letters to the sounds of his own spoken language.

At the prompting of both mother and father, the teachers, reluctantly at first, began to write out simple words and sentences in block letters for Seth to decode. He took to it ferociously, seemingly able to spin the sounds of the letters together so swiftly as to be able to hold them in his memory long enough to realize that it was a word that he was sounding out.

As discovered in some of the attempts a number of years ago (notably those of Omar Khayam Moore) to develop reading machines, the key to such success was a memory of the sounds of the letters and an ability to break down letter combinations into their spoken word equivalents so that the meaning of the word would not be lost. These children had an unusual talent to recognize visual/sound equivalences fast enough to maintain simple meanings.

This actually became a problem for Seth as he moved into kindergarten. Other children were now learning to decode, often making a quiet transition to visual encoding, freeing themselves from the need to hear the sounds put together into words, as Seth still had to do. In fact, their silent reading speeds began to surpass their oral fluency. Seth seemed locked into first grade, in the decoding model. Somehow he found it difficult to free himself from mouthing the sounds that the letters and words resonated through his young mind.

It was a difficult transition into second grade before Seth began a gradual abandonment of the decoding/sounding out approach to reading, to look only at the letters and words, which allowed his automatic visual/featural system to take over in presenting the total word/sentence to his ample intelligence.

Later, his mother admitted that it probably was an error that both parents had made, out of an anxiety that their sons would not learn to read easily, knowing full well the academic as well as the psychological penalty that a nonreader must pay. As Seth's mother would ruefully note, she had too literally accepted some of the more outspoken critics of modern reading instruction, perhaps fearing the reliability of what she had herself learned in her own professional studies. What they misguidedly were searching for was a "sure thing" head start for their sons.

## COMMENTS

There is no such thing as a "sure thing" head start. Reading, like so many other skills and learnings that a child experiences, can be triggered. Ultimately, all learning obeys an inner law of development different in degree and character from child to child.

Some early readers are very bright. Their fluency matches an intelligence that will keep them at the front of the pack. Other early fluent readers will move with the pack, gradually sliding back into the middle of the group as they mature. Then again, many extremely intelligent children will shock and dismay their parents and families, learning to read fluently with difficulty, only in second, sometimes third grade.

A few children will reveal, as did Seth, some unusual skills—an agility to decode rapidly—often fooling us into a belief that they are "really reading." There are many other developmental variations for which parents and teachers should prepare themselves.

On occasion, we see quite young children, four or five years old, who will later turn out to be nonreading dyslectics. At age 4, they seem to be reading with fluency and pleasure. Admittedly the material is simple. Yet because of their ability to utilize the always-plentiful context clues, pictures, or the reading of fellow students in the group, they can persuade us as to their superior reading skills, admittedly with a few "miscue" visual misidentifications of letters and words. Reading problems invariably lie ahead for them.

## YOUNG PROBLEM READERS

For the majority of children, first grade, the six-to-seven-year-old period in a child's life, can be pivotal for their educational destiny. And it will be reading success that will be the most important. By the end of first grade, the parents will get a reasonable sense of their child's destiny, at least short-term.

It may be that the children make it through that "magic moment" during which they begin to see words and sentences as whole units of visual thought, understanding and enjoying what they have encoded. It may be that this has not happened, that even using decoding skills aided by a modest nonrigid phonics program is only helping such children make limited gains toward the goal of happy reading experiences appropriate to their age.

The parent, with the help of the classroom teacher, plus any other resource assistance that might be available in the school system, should then be on the alert to remediate. The question is what kinds of things should a parent look for, at the least as contributing to the information dialogue with the experts, if they are listening.

The two worst things that parents can do are: (1) panic if their child is not reading on a first-grade level by early June, or (2) ignore the evidence, hoping that Johnny or Mary will pick up reading skills in September of second grade (for there are few retentions anymore in our public schools). If I were to pick the worst scenario, it would be the first, the panic situation.

Chances are, such a child's reading system is slow to mature, especially if the child in question is a boy. If the classroom environment is calm and the teacher is attentive and actually putting the children through a systematic reading program, the child should start to move slowly into featural reading, how fast or efficiently depending on the child's maturation rate and intelligence, and ultimately the functionality of the individual reading neurology.

In Chapter 10, I will discuss the Reading Recovery approach laid out by Marie Clay. This is an extremely intensive remedial program directed at first graders who seem to be at risk. The comprehensive battery of techniques that the program offers to bring the children up to grade level is directed both to those children from deprived environments who need to be exposed to basic readiness skills and to middle-class children who are not moving in tandem with their peers in first grade.

## "READING-SYSTEM" IMMATURE

Fred is seven years and four months old. It has been a rocky row to hoe as far as his reading progress is concerned. To be fair, it is not that Fred has a clear reading disability or manifests symptoms of slow learning. He learned all his letters, their sounds, and could at a reasonable five-and-a-half years old put letters together as sounded-out words. His phonics skills were respectable. But here he is, able to sound out words little better than when he was a whole year younger.

Fred writes well from dictation and he is able to make up his own stories. His spelling is fairly good—he never had to use the crutch of invented spelling to keep up with the rest of the class in free writing. Fred is an avid conversationalist, discussing interesting events from baseball to his father's latest real estate deal that was talked about at the dinner table.

He is a bright boy, the teachers told his parents, but he is a slow-to-mature reader. Eventually that inner brain neurology, which has little relationship to other developmental structures in the learning progress of the child, will "hook in," and Fred will one day wake up to a reading binge.

The key to this confidence by the educational professionals was that there were no other blockages that could explain this kind of "retardation." Fred was alert, bright, curious, and put together as a person and a thinker. He could write phonetically quite well, had an effective imagination, and, most importantly, could decode enough to enjoy reading stories as long as most of the words were in regular phonetic spellings.

Give him time, the parents were told. He will come through.


## PERSONALITY IMMATURE

Beryl is another boy. Bright, brash, and somewhat of a pain in the classroom, Beryl wants to play, and to play again, to tease, and sometimes to sass. One doesn't know what to expect of him—a sarcastic comment, a pointed quip, often a truly precocious insight.

But it is impossible to get him to sit still, open a book, and concentrate on the letters and their sounds or meanings. Often he will sit down for a moment and scribble a story chaotically and illegibly onto a large sheet of paper. If he is in the mood, he will wait his turn and read it with his fellow first graders. Ask him to repeat his story five minutes later and the class will hear an entirely different story. Imagination he has.

In a reading group there are definite signs that this six-and-a-half-year-old could put it together. He will begin to sound out a word on the basis of immediately prior instruction in a particular phonic regularity. Almost instantly he will appear to look momentarily and intently at the word in the book, say it, and simultaneously the several words after it that would complete the sentence.

A few minutes later when it is his turn in the group again, he will act like a four-year-old, giggling, acting dumb and unknowing, not to be cajoled into making a serious attempt at learning to read. Mother says that he is the same, at times, at home. Beryl can often be quite obstreperous and "fresh." At other times, he is content to play quietly at a game by himself or with his four-year-old brother.

At this point, Beryl is not interested in systematic reading instruction. Intellectually he is ready. Evidence is that his reading system is mature enough to allow for fluent reading. But he is not yet ready. He needs some time. He is definitely not a candidate for depressant drugs, active as he is in the social atmosphere of the classroom.

He could flourish in a nongraded environment, such as first-through third-grade classroom. That way the school could avoid dispensing the punishment of retention and the belittling experience of being in a class with younger children. Also, the nongraded class would not have the impact of automatic promotion, in which children who are not ready for the work of the class to which they have been promoted are left to float on their own. The teacher can't do everything.

The child whose personality is immature could have some real problems in a nonsympathetic environment where there is little understanding of his peculiarly unique, often male symptomology. Let us hope that he has strong, resourceful parents. He could be a classic "late bloomer."

## READING DISABLED?

Suzy should not have been a surprise to her parents. Uncle Al was notorious for his fumbling spelling and lack of interest in writing or reading. He would prefer to fiddle around with a new electronic toy for hours to make it work, rather than read the assembly directions that came with it.

It was only later that Dad told Mom about his own father's problems with reading, which eventually caused him difficulties as he was building his business. Grandpa was astute enough not to stand on ceremony. He hired marketing managers and a good administrative assistant, after which his business grew.

Perhaps Dad thought that since Suzy was an only child, and especially since she was a girl, this bit of family history could be ignored. For all the females of the clan seemed to be fine and accomplished readers, as he was himself. Also, Suzy's Mom and her family seemed to reveal no reading or writing difficulties. They were all, like his own, a brainy and successful all-American family.

Thus they were unprepared for Suzy's reading and writing hangups, and did not get "on the stick" until it was almost too late. Suzy herself didn't seem to notice the fact that her reading was almost all by context; she often made up some good answers to the silent reading questions that her teacher directed at her. Even the teacher labeled her as an imaginative and intelligent child who seemed to have some spelling and penmanship problems, somewhat unusual for a first-grade female.

True, Suzy was not a good decoder in the beginning stages. Often she did not hear the differences in sound between "m" and "n" or "t" and "d." But because she was so bright and understood that reading was not for merely translating those blurry, waving marks on the page into sounds, but rather for providing interesting stories and information, her mind substituted the sounds that she heard in her inner ear to the letters and words that she was assigned to decode into sound, and then meaning. The result was slow reading, but definitely, even when incorrect, the sentences made sense. Thus the teachers, too, were lulled.

Her writing seemed chaotic. Often she was not able to write her letters straight on the lined paper, from left to right. However, since many first graders do not have the small muscle coordination to write the letters and words clearly, it was thought that Suzy merely represented the physically immature wing of development, more common to boys, in this case unusual but still normal, in this mature and highly intelligent six-year-old female.

The first-grade teacher did not want to panic Suzy's Dad, a prominent local businessman and formerly head of the PTO, and Mom was reference librarian in the local community college. Mother did not express concern at the parent-teacher conferences, especially when the teacher referred to a probable myelination delay in Suzy's reading neurology, this as a probable explanation for the slow development of her fluent reading skills, especially oral reading. Still, this conference was in April, and second grade was beckoning.

**Figure 8.1**
**The Writing of Dyslexic Children**

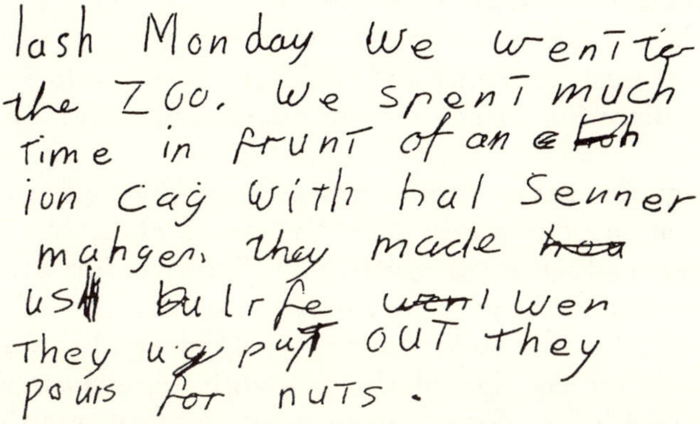

Last Monday we went to the Zoo. We spent much time in front of an iron cage which held seven monkeys. They made us laugh when they put out their paws for nuts.

Writing to dictation. R.G., male aged 11 years.

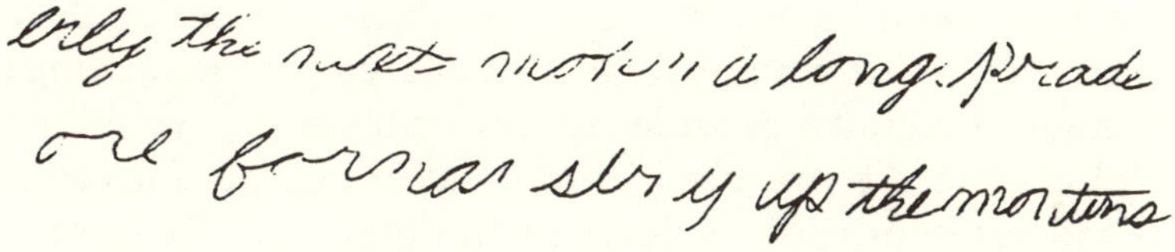

Early the next morning, a long parade of farm animals started up the mountains.

Writing to dictation. R.S., male aged 13 years.

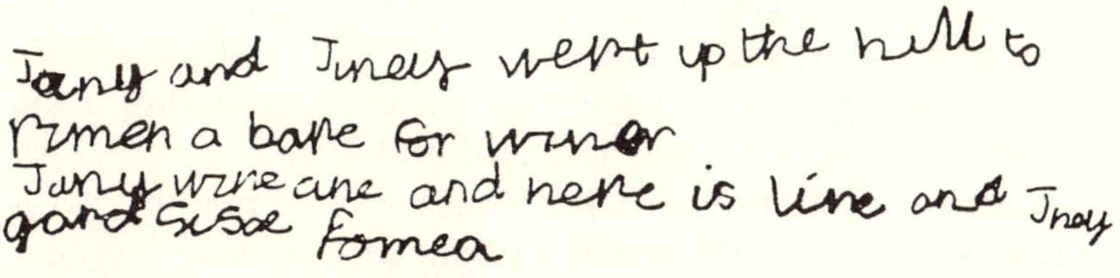

Jack and Jill went up the hill to fetch a pail of water.
Jack fell down and broke his crown, and Jill came tumbling after.

Writing to dictation. J.L., male aged 9 years.

The parents, on their part, were concerned not to panic the school or to throw their considerable political weight around in the name of their own daughter, so they decided to bear and forebear. They worked at home with Suzy, making an attempt to introduce new and interesting books and children's magazines to her that might stimulate her interest. Progress seemed slow. And then it was June.

Second grade was a wholly new setting. The new teacher saw quickly that, as compared with the other children, Suzy was winging her reading. Writing was only slightly better, and spelling was still a disaster. Suzy's parents were alerted, and the district reading specialist was called in for a preliminary diagnosis.

Suzy could manage her math work with relative ease; she was on the high side of the class average, except when it came to reading the verbals. In reviewing her record, it was clear that she had excelled in number concepts since kindergarten and the readiness tests, where she had shown superior achievement. This had led the teachers somewhat astray, since math concepts were good predictors at that stage of a child's future fluent reading abilities, involving prediction and integration of reading material. Yet the fluent reading didn't happen.

Suzy might well have a clinically established reading disability and thus be eligible for some high-level analysis at the reading clinic of the state university. A wide battery of tests of psycholinguistic skills plus others more clinical and neurological ultimately did reveal the symptoms of dyslexia in the making. The question of instruction now loomed large.

As the specialist from the reading clinic explained in the report to the parents and the school, the instructional pathway should lie along those lines laid down two decades ago by the famed Dr. Joseph Wepman of the University of Chicago, in his "modality program." This was to find those sensory-perceptual pathways that Suzy found to be the easiest to follow in learning.

These might be in math and in oral verbal development. In the reading and writing area, a shift to a more phonic/linguistic approach, with slower decoding and skill-building, was called for. All these programs would require a highly disciplined reading structure.

For example, such skill building might involve tracing the letter shapes as Suzy read, or masking that part of the page under the actual lines that she would be reading. Such slow, sequential instruction could both discipline her mind and guide her eyes.

But always, the Wepman theme was *not* to attempt a remediation of the modality that was acting as the blockade for her learning. Suzy needed to bring all the information that she was getting in the learning process to deep structure, to understanding and meaning, and to do this in any way possible. Even the piano lessons that she was now receiving at home might help her, since they involved reading abstract musical notation and coordinating hand and eye with her musical ear and feeling.

As the district specialist later explained both to the parents and the classroom teacher, no one could predict what strategies Suzy would devise for herself, spontaneously from within herself, to obtain the necessary information from the reading material that would lead to understanding. These are the quiet mysteries to be revealed in a young mind at work, intent on learning.

The overriding need was for teacher and family to work continuously on the task of inundating Suzy with various forms of literacy exposure, always trying out new skill experiences, writing or reading poetry, logic games, and computer programs appropriate to her age. Any one or all of these could trigger a positive response and thus offer a clue that might become a breakthrough point in the fluent reading process.

The plan must be to test the weak modality constantly, in this case the purely visual/featural skill of reading-skimming-understanding. Test this modality with minimal amounts of visual information from the reading texts. But don't overdo the corrections and remediation if Suzy is not quick to respond positively—in achievement. Be patient, for so often, as with the neurologically immature, all systems could come into a place in a moment. If this does not happen, she might spontaneously or through instruction find an alternate pathway to reading as a rapid decoder.

But then, a tilt of the head, even a set of new-fangled tinted lenses might become the first step in a process of gradual literacy empowerment and reading fluency. Progress, can be made to the point of allowing that hungry brain to achieve its desires for competence and knowledge. Good luck, Suzy!

## THE SLOW READER

Mark is a slow reader, and causes despair to his family. But not to himself. This adds to his parents' frustration and trauma. Dad is a hard-driving sales executive for a furniture manufacturer; Mom is a registered nurse. Amy is three years Mark's junior and a pin-bright delight to all, including Mark, whose love is duly reciprocated by his sister.

Mark was slow to talk and slow to walk and run. For the first four years of Mark's life, his parents calmed each other with the homily that "fast to trot, first to rot" would ensure Mark's long-run achievement even if at first he took his time. A warm-hearted preschool teacher did express concern that Mark had trouble relating to the other children because he was lethargic in his play, class responses, and interactions. The children, unless controlled by the teachers, tended to make fun of him, often taunting him for his indifference to acting and reacting.

By kindergarten and the first literacy learnings—the alphabet and its sounds, the choral readings, the "draw a man" contests, the arts and crafts work—Mark had not yet displayed that bit of spark in any area of learning and play that might indicate readiness—verbal ripostes, kidding around, teasing, imaginative story-telling, or even delight in memory games involving letter sounds. Many skills came to him modestly, and eventually. But everything seemed difficult.

Still Mark entered a regular first-grade class since the wise kindergarten teacher did not want to preempt nature, as she put it. Mark could make a breakout in first grade. The help he received at home had given a semblance of the reading readiness skills that he needed. At age six he might speed forward as the recalcitrant neurology finally made its connections.

Quietly, without attracting attention to Mark by the other children, a program was carefully put into place, consisting of decoding phonics, word analysis, personal verbal expression, copying, and workbook skills. Through this, Mark was drawn along in the first-grade curriculum. By the end of first grade he could read, ever so slowly, and although with much forgetting of earlier-read materials, he could obtain some comprehension and enjoyment of words and sentences. It was clear that what was observable in his first-grade and then second-grade reading achievements was duplicated in other areas of the elementary curriculum.

By second grade, several specialists in the school were brought in and the possibility of entering Mark into a district-wide special education program now became real. The increasingly troubled parents were told that Mark gave all the appearances of having a mild retardation problem, equivalent to an IQ in the 80s range. (He was yet too young for these tests to be more than an approximation.) But he was certainly educable, and with his rather phlegmatic, even happy personality, it was probable that in maturity he could hold down an unskilled job with responsibility and success.

Watch him carefully as he moves into adolescence, the psychologists advised Mark's parents. The new biology of pubescence sometimes opens up a vast cauldron of unexpected energies. And unless Mark's intellectual potentialities likewise spurted upward, there could occur the disasters that we see today in many children whose energies, both sexual and physical, are undimmed. But these youngsters are intellectually incapable of controlling and disciplining their behavior. In Mark's case, such a dangerous development was unlikely to occur.

In the meantime, Mark would need regular and intense instruction in the various skills of reading. These would probably involve both decoding and slow "fluent" reading, if, by the end of second grade he could recognize the shape of words, and identify the meanings of uncomplicated words.

Mark's math skills were as yet rudimentary. But they could be made functional. It was not a serious learning problem, since only children below 70 IQ are usually labeled as clinically retarded—in some cases such children are unable to care for themselves in the usual social settings—as compared with those with IQs in the low normal range of children, such as Mark.

Mark showed no other overt characteristics of being retarded, except that he was slow of response in all his academic and life activities. He could be taught to read simple materials, learn to find his way around the city, even be able to write and fill out simple application forms. But it would have to be a very concrete and guided educational program. What he wasn't taught in school or home he was unlikely to pick up himself, as much brighter children often did. Their experiences anywhere and everywhere were learning opportunities. Mark would be different.

All in all, Mark, unknown to himself, seemingly had caused a family to become extremely distressed. Their dreams for the future, their hopes and wishes, were dashed. The teachers could only wish them luck in staying together. Lovely Mark, barely aware of the outside pain, could only assume that the smiles and good wishes truly represented the full reality of his blurred world.

## THE GIFTED CHILD

What a surprise it was for this child to be gifted. His father, a well-known serious actor, had met his mother at a drama festival. The father was unable to marry the mother when the pregnancy was discovered. He had previous commitments. She decided to carry Dominick to term. She was a practicing psychiatrist and found the anticipation of motherhood to be pleasant, especially because of her relatively advanced age and her economic well-being.

Thus Dominick became a wanted child of a single mother, soon well-accustomed to being in the care of various nannies and sitters. In fact it was one of these nannies who alerted the mother to Dominick's odd behavior. When this nanny talked playfully to little six-month-old Dominick as she attended to household duties, describing the furniture, clock hours, and other objects about his room, he would invariably look searchingly at the object that she described and make sounds that sounded eerily as if he wanted the nanny to answer his own questions about the room, the world.

When he became one year old, words came, and soon thereafter sentences, and then the "picked-up" preternaturally mature vocabulary. Yet he did not begin walking until he was fourteen months old. Shortly after his second birthday, Dominick was sent to nursery school. It was clear to all that this was a bright, alert child. He had grown to be quite sturdy, as well. His mother's friends all advised her to go slowly with his education, enrich rather than advance was their advice. And she listened.

Dominick had trouble in school. Even though he was not a truly fluent reader until well into his sixth year, his decoding and contextual skills outran the primers of his fellow first graders. His math skills were phenomenally mature. In kindergarten, except for the test on shape matching and "draw a man" maturity skills, his scores were "off the charts." When he began to read fluently and then independently, toward the end of first grade and then into second, teachers could not feed him enough material, at the least to keep him quiet—he often interrupted the class, kindly volunteering answers to anything that anyone had trouble with, including the teacher. By third grade, Dominick was reading junior-high material, enjoying it phenomenally, and asking questions that pushed the teachers to the limits of their knowledge.

By this time, Dominick's mother was seriously considering taking him out of the fine local elementary school, even though it was suffused with children of various professional, middle-class backgrounds. Dominick was getting violin lessons at home, as well as participating in various sports activities and in the Boy Scouts. His written compositions in school and the letters he wrote to uncles, aunts, and cousins were exceptionally mature and put together, with no signs of any weak areas of achievement.

A conference with a professor in the education of the gifted at the state university helped to focus his mother's thinking about Dominick's education and future. The professor's suggestion was simple: "Keep him with his friends in his present school." Truthfully, the children were not at all put off by Dominick's brilliant aggressiveness. They thought he was both special and fun, the rational response one might expect from all healthy children, a deference to the differences in all of us.

The professor advised her to keep Dominick reading and writing, and advancing his math skills, along with all the other enrichment activities, music, and sports, in which Dominick remained eager to participate. Make sure that his brilliant mind does not outrun his skills in the various fundamentals, including the three Rs. The goal should be that Dominick arrive at secondary school adolescence with all his skills honed and his mind and eagerness intact.

The secondary school experience, the professor admonished, is the key to Dominick's future. That is where his mother should place her most careful investment. The mind grows to maturity early in puberty. A fine, rigorous, and serious secondary school education could prepare Dominick to attain the finest higher educational achievements, no matter which college or university program he might choose.

We will never learn where Dominick's talents really lie if we do not challenge him in junior and senior high school. Elementary schooling should be considered to be an important but not crucial preparatory experience. It should provide a chance to learn, but also the chance to be free to suffer the joys of childhood, not to be turned into a well-oiled academic puppet.

The professor further warned that many changes occur during puberty, not the least the transformation of many incipient little geniuses into ordinary teenagers. Conversely, some ordinary, middling elementary students become blazing novas of creativity with the coming of intellectual maturity. Why, who, when? Here is the mystery of being human.

Dominick was a precious talent that had to be nurtured. In the end, all the educators admonished, to a still-astonished mother, it is what is inside that human being that will come out and make itself known. Then, it will be out of all of our hands. We will just have to stand back and let him show his stuff.

## THE BORED AND UNINTERESTED

Both guidance counselors and teachers were concerned. Even the elementary school principal was called in for his thoughts about Helen. The principal recognized that a legal suit was one day possible because of the lack of systematic instruction that could be laid at the feet of the teachers and counselors. Helen was not an unusual exemplar of a child who didn't want to learn, but the solution may have broached the borderlines of educational malfeasance.

True, Helen's mother had sought to sweep the problem of her middle child under the rug, with the comment, "We are plain old blue-color folks." It could have been an easy out for the teachers to let Helen drift. But there was more to the story than a child who didn't want to learn, who used all of her wits to avoid responsibilities, to dream, to wander about the school when she was excused to go to the girls bathroom.

Helen seemed quite capable when she wanted to learn. On several occasions she had whipped through workbook material both in arithmetic and phonics so that she could go out for recess, and did the work perfectly, as if to "show them." At other times, Helen turned in papers that the first-grade teacher found impossible to correct. When asked to do some creative writing about events, descriptions, or dreams, she wrote nothing. She dawdled and seemed distracted.

The cause of Helen's incipient reading and academic failure, here at the threshold of second grade, was attributed to Helen's dysfunctional home. Her father had several times abandoned his wife and three children to go off, somewhere, only to return, to regain his unskilled custodial job at the local window frame factory. Once again, he begged for and received forgiveness from his family.

This was a man who once could handle skilled mechanical jobs had he not had his weaknesses.

The wife and mother of three took a job as a supermarket cashier to keep the family off welfare. But there was enormous conflict and chaos in this home. The older son, Charles, already had a checkered academic career, a reputation as a fifth-grade hell-raiser. Yet the consensus of his teachers was that he was not a dull student and could do well when his heart was in it. Charles seemed more of a survivor than Helen, who seemed headed toward massive failure because her mind could not as yet be channeled into reasonable efforts to learn to read or do any academic work.

The teachers were willing to take a chance on the family, that they would not interfere with the school strategy, in a sense "calling them" on their seeming neglect of Helen. It was their guess that what this child needed was an environment without the stressful din and pressures generated in that chaotic three-room apartment into which the family was all squashed. (In addition to all the other distractions mentioned above, two television sets blared day and night in the home.) No sensitive or intelligent human could survive such circumstances without an act of mental disengagement, to crawl into one's deepest reserves of privacy and aloneness.

This was Helen, and if school was ever to serve her to become a learner, reader, and survivor, then, the teachers and counselors reasoned, they had to "lay off." This meant tempting her intellectually only on occasion and in subtle ways. But most of all, they viewed her classroom hours as a precious time for renewal. Perhaps at some moment they could expect Helen to crawl out of herself and engage in her own forms of mental empowerment. If the school retained its coherence of purpose and consistency of response, then perhaps in second grade, or at sometime beyond, Helen might try to venture out and seek help from a teacher who, hopefully, would be there to assist, but not to enforce.

There are an infinite variety of unique children that every parent and teacher will have to confront. View the examples given above as only a sample of the challenges that young human beings will place before the old. Good luck, be wise. Remember that the earlier we understand their uniqueness, the more likely we will be able to help children make the most of themselves.

# Chapter 9

# *Whole Language: Caution*

The ideas of the whole language movement offer much that is worthwhile, which will become evident as I describe the arguments of the movement's proponents. But it is important to add a measure of extreme caution here, because its advocates, as in too many educational movements, take on a zealous, almost messianic attitude that bodes no criticism, not even sober evaluation.

Later in this chapter I will amplify on two cautionary criticisms of the unlimited claims of some of the whole language movement's advocates. They are serious concerns, which when fairly evaluated will tarnish the gild on this lily:

1. When it is applied to real children, not children in the abstract, the whole language approach to reading instruction presents a number of impracticalities—whole language does not work in practice for an ever-increasing proportion of young children in the beginning stages of reading.

2. There is in whole language advocacy a real theoretical error that strikes at the heart of the rationalization for teaching reading. This error lies in blurring the difference between learning to speak and learning to read. The error is rooted in the virtual ignoring of the existence in each child's developmental make-up of the *reading system*. Before a child will be ready to benefit fully from a good whole language program, she must surmount this maturational and educational hurdle.

## BASIC CLAIMS OF WHOLE LANGUAGE

Whole language is a fairly new educational movement in reading instruction. Thus, it needs to be defined and described. Kenneth Goodman, a specialist in reading, was an early convert and leader in the meaning emphasis tradition initially given impetus by the research into psycholinguistics. With the realization that this scientific work did not clearly spell out any special pedagogical or programmatic methodology in the teaching of reading, Goodman became a leader of the whole language movement in reading education:

> Many school traditions seem to have actually hindered language development. In our zeal to make it easy, we've made it hard . . . primarily by breaking whole (natural) language up into bite-size, but abstract little pieces. We took apart the language and turned it into words, syllables, and isolated sounds. Unfortunately we also postponed its natural purpose—the communication of meaning—and turned it into a set of abstractions, unrelated to the needs and experiences of the children we sought to help.[1]

What Goodman is clearly protesting is the kind of phonic analysis of sounds, phonemes, and word identification that takes place in early reading. He feels that not enough attention is given in the classroom, at the time of early reading and after, to the meaning and concept identification that reading shares with other dimensions of language, including the natural spoken language.

The next descriptive quote is not from a wholly persuaded advocate:

Whole language means teaching reading in a whole-language arts context. It establishes an environment where the emphasis is on meaning; where learners are viewed as active experience-seekers and decision-makers; where learning is thought to be transformative rather than simply additive; where molar units are emphasized and where the whole (reading) is not simply the aggregate of skills or strategies; and where the teacher is thought of as a guide, facilitator, and collaborator.[2]

The basic claim of the advocates of whole language could be stated as follows: Since all children naturally acquire spoken language without any external "teaching" by the adult world, merely by being immersed in a rich linguistic environment of speaking humans, the same natural process should take place when the child is exposed to the visual written version of language.

As such, whole language advocates argue that the first obligation of teachers is to unify both language by ear and language by sight, in an educational environment that is suffused with language in all forms. Especially, they do not want to engage in the artificial divisions of the oral versus written language experiences. They should all come together in the most "natural" pedagogical manner.

## REDEEMING THE LEARNER

The unnatural is therefore the enemy. Who are these falsifiers of the truths of linguistic learning? They are, of course, the phonics advocates, in the main. But there are others, some of whom might prove surprising to anyone with some historical awareness of previous panaceas in reading education. So, too—if you have followed the reading wars over the decades—there will be seemingly "good guys" who are now shown to be in error.

Phonics teaching, in any sense, rule-bound or not, is seen as a serious perversion of the natural reading process. The kinds of specific awareness into which we presumably induct the pre-schooler, such as the relation between the sounds that can be assigned to letters and syllables, would be ruled out. The slow decoding of reading that goes on in the early stages of the elementary grades is also rejected.

**Figure 9.1**
**Whole Language Instruction: Letter to Students Explaining the Reading Journal**

Dear Students,

Welcome back from your summer vacations! As part of your reading class this year, we're going to try something different which you may not have done in previous grades. Each of us is going to keep a Reading Journal.

What is the Reading Journal all about? The Journal is a place where you will be able to write about the books that you will be reading throughout the year in my class. In the Journal, you will write letters to me or to other students in the class.

What will the letters be about? You can write anything you want about the book you are reading. You can express your thoughts, your feelings, or your reactions. How do you feel about the book? What does the book make you think about? What do you like or dislike about it? What's the story about? Who are the characters? Can you relate to their problems? Will the person you are writing to like the book? What does the story mean to you?

When you finish writing your new entry, place your journal on my desk or the desk of the student you are writing to. When I or a classmate receive your letter, we will be able to write back to you in your Journal.

Here are some simple guidelines to follow to make sure that the Reading Journal is a success:

1. You may write as many letters as you wish, but at least one letter each week.

2. If you receive a letter from a classmate, respond to it by the next day.

3. Make sure you date each letter and mention the name of the book you are reading.

I will explain other details about the Reading Journal in class. You will have plenty of class time to write your letters. I hope that you are as excited as I am by the prospects of sharing what you are reading. The Reading Journal will be a great way to help us explore what we are feeling and thinking about the books that we are reading.

Happy reading! Happy writing!

Sincerely,

*Mrs. Burns*

*Source:* Excerpt from *Case Studies in Whole Language* by Richard T. Vacca and Timothy V. Rasinski, copyright © 1992 by Holt, Rinehart and Winston, Inc. Reprinted by permission of the publisher.

**Figure 9.2**
**Whole Language Instruction: Student Letters Evaluating the Reading Program**

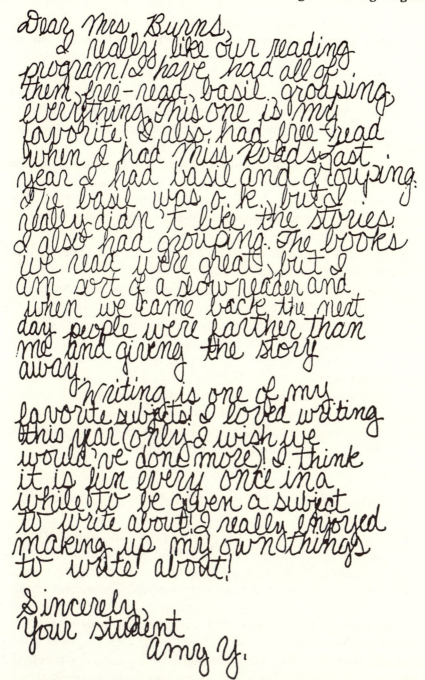

Dear Mrs. Burns,

I really like our reading program! I have had all of them, free-read, basil, grouping, everything. This one is my favorite! I also had free-read when I had Miss Roads. Last year I had basil and grouping. The basil was o.k., but I really didn't like the stories. I also had grouping. The books we read were great, but I am sort of a slow reader and when we came back the next day people were farther than me and giving the story away.

Writing is one of my favorite subjects! I loved writing this year (only I wish we would've done more)! I think it is fun every once in a while to be given a subject to write about! I really enjoyed making up my own things to write about!

Sincerely,
Your student
Amy Y.

*Source:* Excerpt from *Case Studies in Whole Language* by Richard T. Vacca and Timothy V. Rasinski, copyright © 1992 by Holt, Rinehart and Winston, Inc. Reprinted by permission of the publisher.

The view is that such teaching interferes with the natural flow of written language awareness in the child. Where the phonics advocates even in their most watered-down claims argue that the child must become aware of the alphabetic principle, in the making of our written language, and that the child must learn the equivalences between speech sounds and at least some of the regularities mirrored in writing, the whole language leadership is not persuaded.

They argue that an immersion in books, having the teacher read to children and having them write their own personal stories, even using "invented spelling," will allow children to slip naturally into a reading/writing mode, to learn to love reading without the tedious artificiality of phonics.

In general, analysis of the parts of speech, drills in spelling, study of letter/sound beginnings and endings in words, all those supposedly skill-building techniques to which we expose children in order to acquaint them with the workings of the written language as it builds on the natural spoken forms, are likewise rejected as educational tools. So, too, is the teaching of the parts of speech and syntactic analysis as to how sentences and ideas are constructed in reading and writing.

The argument is that such drill and technical skill building fragments the learning process, possibly turning the child away from the true learning attitude, the desire to read whole books, and the ability to grasp whole ideas and meaning.

## HISTORY REPEATED?

What is also interesting is the seeming rejection of the venerable progressive education advocacy of whole word identification, the look-say method of teaching reading. For many years, look-say and rule-bound phonics instruction were engaged in mortal combat. This earlier stage in the reading wars, which in the United States can be traced back to the mid-nineteenth century, eventually dredged up political overtones. Here conservatives urged a back-to-basics teaching of reading through the phonics approach. The look-say, whole-word identification method unfortunately suffered from "left-wing" associations, and in the end eventually disappeared from commercial basal reading series.

Whole language advocates view whole word identification, in which first-grade teachers strove to develop in children a sight vocabulary of a certain number of words that could be identified and understood without phonic analysis, as part of the problem of language fragmentation. They feel that words should never be studied out of context of books and stories.

By teaching children to look for meaning in stories, through both spoken story telling as well as the oral and silent reading of stories, children will recognize words as part of the entire context of a story. One can argue that just as children learn the meaning of words in the natural language by hearing them in context, and almost spontaneously speak these words, then, in context, make sentences, so, too, the same process of learning will apply in the written medium in the reading process.

The larger artificiality created by a reading program oriented toward skill building is its inevitable division of the four dimensions of language, speech, listening, reading, and writing, into discrete areas of teaching and learning. In our zeal to build competency, so the whole language people argue, we tend to separate contextually the natural manner in which these language dimensions flow into each other and reinforce language competency in general.

Note the resemblance of whole language rhetoric to the progressive educators' previously fashionable project method approach to the elementary and high school curriculum. Here, subject matters such as math, social studies, language learning, the arts, and science all came together as students involved themselves in real life projects. Life isn't divided into subject matters, so argued the great progressivist, William Heard Kilpatrick. Children learn what they live, and they should live what they learn, he espoused.

So, too, in reading. Reading is part of language, argue whole language teachers. Never teach it apart from the way it interacts with writing, speaking, and listening. Teaching reading in reading groups and through reading exercises apart from the rest of language learning results in a serious distortion for the child. The boredom and lack of interest that was discussed in the previous chapter can be attributed, according to the whole language advocates, at least partly to the fragmentation of teaching, which confuses and shuts out the child.

## "DUMBING DOWN"

One final contemporary rejection by whole language advocates is especially interesting. These are the "readability indices" that guided the writing of basals and other graded reading materials. The criteria of readability were vocabulary and syntactic complexity, keeping the words simple enough and the sentences pretty much declarative, that is, without complex modifying clauses or constructions.

The rationale for the concern with readability as it developed in the early 1980s was the disappointing result of the original push for *meaning*, which was a product of the psycholinguistic revolution of the 1970s. It turned out that the instructional readers then produced were much too complex in meaning and sentence structure for the children they were prepared for. A meaning emphasis, it turned out, was too great a challenge for the average elementary-school reader.

Then, it was almost as if a U-turn was made in reading education. Soon, the journals were packed with articles about the various criteria that now ought to be used in writing texts for children. Don't overburden the children with big words and complicated sentences. As Albert Shanker, president of the American Federation of Teachers, the teachers' union, put it, this was a part of the educational "dumbing down of America" that had begun in the 1970s, and was now reflected in all textbooks, elementary through the high school. Also, it was probably involved in the slide of our college-bound students' SAT scores.

Whole language advocates, realizing what had resulted from this aborted scientific revolution and fairly—as it now seems—attempted to reverse this trend. They advocated, without mandating any special vocabulary or syntactic patterns in instructional reading materials, that the schools return to a meaning orientation. By allowing for the introduction of the child into all the language modalities, it was hoped that we, parents and teachers, would see a natural rise in vocabulary and story structure sophistication in the child.

But now it would not be achieved by artificial formulas, but by the spontaneous absorption of language learning in the child's exposure to literature and not straight-jacket basals put out by the money-grubbing textbook publishers.

## THE WHOLE LANGUAGE PATH

We have already referred to many of the whole language approaches, especially as they contradict previous teaching assumptions. But it might be useful to summarize them, particularly noting that this philosophy is not a strict method, but an attitude and directionality that should infuse the inner logic of a language/reading program and stimulate a real purposiveness to all the practices of the teacher and the school.

### Emerging Literacy

It is an error to view the process of learning to read as beginning with skill-building readiness. Rather, the term *emerging literacy* is a more accurate description of how a child learns. Simply, the process should be relatively seamless, as in the learning of speech by the infant and young child.

*Immersion* is a term that aptly describes the process used by whole language teachers to facilitate the child's progress from language as speech and listening, to language as reading and writing. By being absorbed in books and language, by always interacting in speech and appreciation, the child will begin to understand what is involved in reading—the meaning and ideas that lie between the covers of a book, the fascination, the lure.

We must take a holistic view both of the child as a living organism and of the process of learning to read and write. The concentration on mechanical skill improvement, whether it be phonics, word analysis, grammar, pronunciation, or spelling, takes the child down a completely different and precarious route of self-development from what is congruent with her inner emergence as a thinker through language.

The teacher becomes a guide and facilitator, always eager to help the children to initiate, using their curiosity and desire to learn, new books and materials, and writing and thinking projects that will elicit the natural growth of vocabulary and both verbal and written expression. Children are not mere subjects in whole language activities, but primary activators of their own sense of discovery. No automatic repetitions, memorizations, or mechanical processes of learning should be used.

Every language activity that the classroom teacher and the children undertake should have a reason. Reading should always promote the further emergence of depth of understanding, pleasure, and the satisfactions that come with competency in all areas of literacy development. The principle is to involve context and the utilization of the four dimensions of language.


## Reading Materials

Every important perspective on the "how" and "why" of the reading process must eventually deal with the books and other materials that the school will offer. Therefore, let us deal with the question of reading materials.

Here the whole language advocates are very clear. For one, the traditional basal reader must be avoided. The basal has always oriented itself toward teachers' mainline concern for building skills, whether these be with controlled sight vocabularies of the word identification type or programs in which the stories have phonetically controlled vocabularies, all presented tediously, step by step.

Basal reading series also come with fill-in-the-blanks, multiple choice workbooks. These are unfortunately usually used by teachers as "busy work" activities, so that teachers can attend to other children, as in reading groups, or take a moment to prepare a lesson in another subject area. Whole language advocates, along with veteran purists, oppose workbook/ditto-machine teaching as mechanical, providing little intellectual stimulation for the child.

The basal approach requires much teacher guidance. It is stereotyped through teachers' editions that suggest the kinds of questions that the teacher should ask about the basal stories, and present exercises and other activities that the authors of the basals feel to be effective. Most educators feel that such teacher prompting might be useful for novice teachers in their first or second year in the classroom. However, such programs of reading development hinder the creativity of the classroom, and stifle any response from the child or teacher that is not preprogrammed in the text.

Literature and individualized reading are the substance of a whole language reading program. Literature means books written at the appropriate age levels of the child but having genuine substance and art compared to the skill-building materials one finds in basals.

Many catalogues are available today to schools and teachers that list books for children by appropriate age levels, books that have been adjudged by experts in the area of children's literature to be worthwhile, whether or not they are Caldecott Award winners. In fact, the resources for children of every age are virtually unlimited, and the cost no greater than what is expended yearly for basals along with their associated workbooks and other materials.

## Pedagogy

Inevitably, we must turn to the question of the pedagogical method favored by whole language enthusiasts. Here we find an individualized reading program, wherein teacher and pupil join in the choice of reading materials of appropriate challenge and interest. This requires of the teacher enormous expenditures of time and record keeping to track the child's accomplishments and trajectory of progress.

At the same time, the child does not remain isolated, as the teacher will bring the children together in groups or as a class to discuss their readings or the written compositions that have been stimulated by the reading. They will share much of their individuality with other classmates, all reinforcing the inner autonomy of purpose and understanding that is the goal of whole language learning. In the above educational environment, the successes should outnumber the failures by a wide margin.

## DREAMS OF EDEN

> Whole language, in particular, seems to say that a good heart goes a long way, and the less teaching the better. It fears structure more than no learning. Its major concern is that the higher cognitive processes be used in reading right from the start, and it flees from the idea that there may be basics to be learned first.[3]

The wine that whole language represents is a well-aged ideal of the romantic mind. What is new is, as always, the particular linguistic clothing, the bottle outside which contains this rich nostalgic tradition.

**Figure 9.3**
**A Third-Grade Writer's Journal**

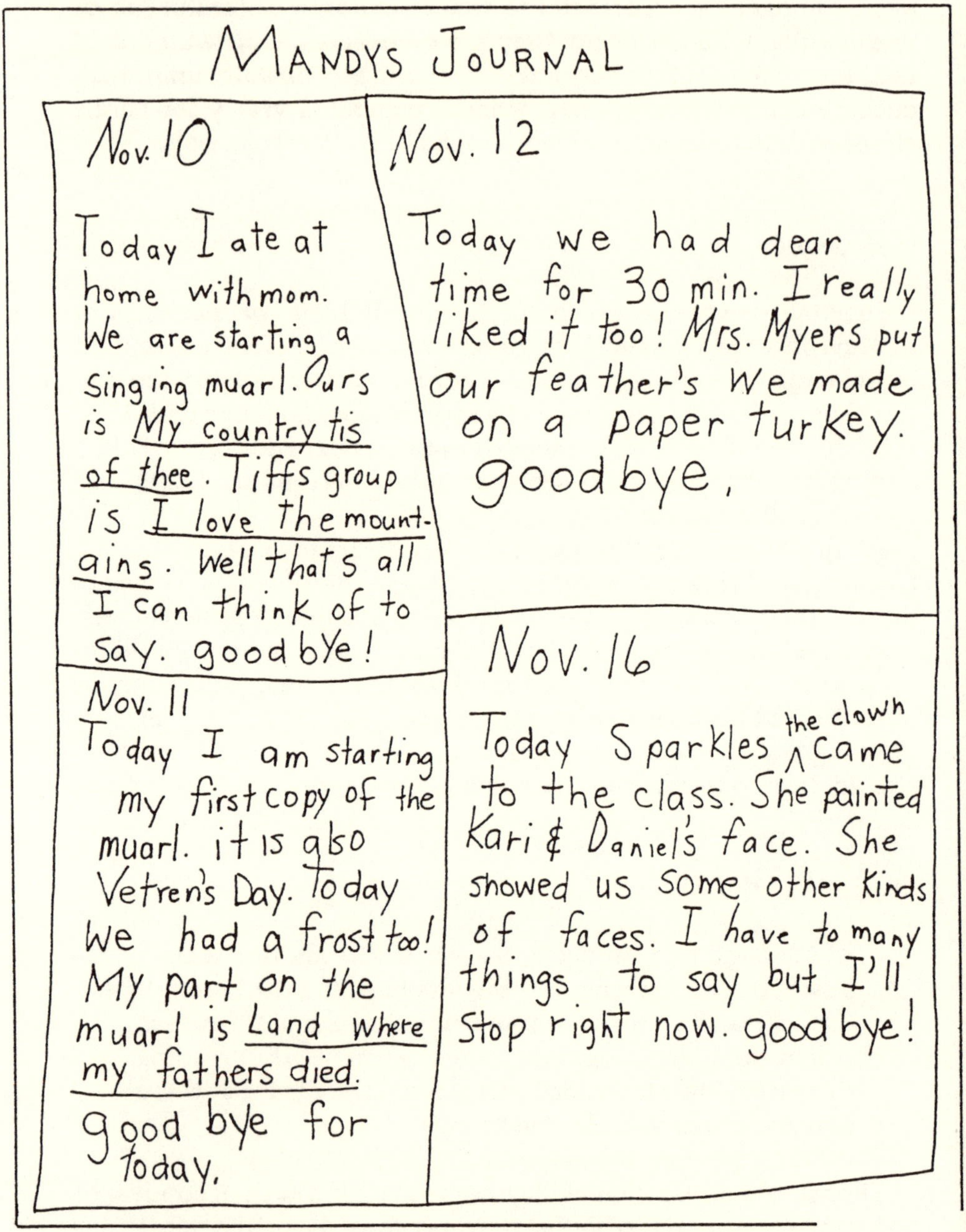

MANDY'S JOURNAL

Nov. 10

Today I ate at home with mom. We are starting a singing muarl. Ours is <u>My country tis of thee</u>. Tiffs group is <u>I love the mount-ains</u>. Well thats all I can think of to say. good bye!

Nov. 11

Today I am starting my first copy of the muarl. it is also Vetren's Day. Today we had a frost too! My part on the muarl is <u>Land where my fathers died.</u> good bye for today.

Nov. 12

Today we had dear time for 30 min. I really liked it too! Mrs. Myers put our feather's we made on a paper turkey. goodbye,

Nov. 16

Today Sparkles the clown came to the class. She painted Kari & Daniel's face. She showed us some other kinds of faces. I have to many things to say but I'll stop right now. good bye!

*Source: Teaching Writing Balance Process and Product* by Gail Tompkins, copyright © 1994. Reprinted by permission of Prentice-Hall, Inc., Upper Saddle River.

Educators since the time of Jean-Jacques Rousseau and his *Émile* have asked themselves and the world, What if? What if we placed a child in the most ideal circumstances, educated her to a vision of utopian possibility without having her contend with the dross of the world? Friedrich Froebel attempted this in the mid-nineteenth century when he created the kindergarten. Here, very young children could play and learn under an all-encompassing religious unity of God's goodness.

The progressivists in the United States turned this into a secular ideal generally promoting the scientific study of humans, teaching children according to their bio-social needs. The idea was pioneered toward the end of the last century at the Francis Parker School in Chicago. Led by the visionary Parker, a veteran leader and hero of the Civil War, this school was the first to involve children actively in the study of the natural world in terms of their developmental stages.

Parker, along with John Dewey, the philosophical godfather of progressive education, and then William Heard Kilpatrick, who gave the project method its national reputation in the public schools, gave teachers hope to go beyond "sit-still" rote learning, with its rigid curricula and stifled, over-disciplined children.

In the 1920s, the heyday of progressive education, teachers such as Mabel Cooke, also from this Chicago hotbed of child centeredness, added the term "the experience curriculum." So it has gone with the Free School, the Open Classroom, and the many romantic visions as to how teaching and learning ought to progress if only the dark forces of reaction would not block the pathways of human aspiration.

Before whole language was the whole-word, sight approach to the teaching of reading. More recently and hardly distinguishable from whole language is the so-called Language Experience Approach (LEA). Emerald Dechant defines LEA as follows:

> What I can think about, I can talk about. What I can say, I can write. What I can write, I can read. I can read what others write for me to read. . . . In LEA, children talk about their experiences, the teacher writes the anecdotal description on the blackboard or records it on an "experience chart," and the children then read what they spoke and the teacher wrote.[4]

LEA was a strong influence on the teaching of reading for about a decade, up into the mid-1980s, when whole language began to be discussed in various reading conferences, journal articles, and then books. However, as any one can see from the above quote, what appears to be unique in LEA is really only phraseology. Probably, teachers since the late 1890s in Francis Parker's experimental school and then throughout the United States and the world have been using such techniques.

One hundred years earlier, during the Napoleonic Wars, in the abandoned convent at Stanz in Switzerland, the saintly Heinrich Pestalozzi taught his seventy orphaned wards. One could argue that he used a version of the experience curriculum, LEA, and whole language teaching, if only from the necessities of the circumstances.

Carol Edelsky, a whole language activist, has argued that the differences between LEA and whole language are largely theoretical. These differences, however, do give rise to certain pedagogical emphases that result in real practical diversity in the teaching of reading in the classroom.

For one, the older LEA approach was based on the view that writing is an outgrowth of thinking about the words that one speaks. Thus, speech has priority over writing. This gives rise to much teacher and student dictation of stories, perhaps to deepen and objectify the oral dimension before it is transcribed into written form.

The transcription of the oral into the written word leads, according to Edelsky, to a view that reading is a secondary skill that must be analyzed as to its grammatical, parts of speech, and punctuation dimensions. According to whole language theory, both reading and writing are independent and parallel with the oral forms of language. These can be studied in and of themselves to obtain different but equally primary forms of language expression.

What Edelsky argues about the theoretical equality of the written forms of language with the oral forms is, of course, correct. And even though the LEA approach was enthusiastically child-centered and freed the reading program from rigid grouping and basal reader approaches, it was, so argues Edelsky, theoretically naive. It did not account for the possibilities of the four modalities of language for producing parallel, if separate, "visions" of the experience of language.

With the theoretical sophistication that the whole language advocates have adopted has come a series of pedagogical conclusions as to how the reading acquisition process takes place in the child. These are highly controversial.

The question we must face during all these new waves of educational enthusiasm is how real is the theory both for the children who are on the receiving end of these "new" discoveries and for the world in which this form of education must take place? It is a question of truth and reality versus the "Garden of Eden" visions of educators too often distanced from the grim world by their hopes.

Sometimes, as with classical look-say, whole-word reading, a core of empirical scientific evidence supports the new curricula and basals that were built around the theory. But then, in the 1950s and 1960s, new realities began to reveal themselves. The practice was less and less successful for the average American student entering the early grades. Since that time, we have been on a roller coaster of high expectations and disillusioned hopes.

## CRITIQUE

I am going to integrate the two main lines of criticism of whole language teaching of reading that I suggested at the beginning of this chapter. This is because I believe that the theoretical myopia of the whole language enthusiasts leads to the practical obliviousness that many parents and teachers encounter when they suggest that all is not as promised when children are immersed in the warm bath of whole language.

What is missing from whole language is the reading system, discussed in Chapter 5. In the view of whole language advocates, immersing (their word) children in the totality of written print materials, texts, newspapers, literature, bus schedules, ads, and the like will have the same effect as immersing children in the world of spoken language. We repeat the question: With total immersion and without specific instruction, is every child sure to learn to read?

The realities of the developmental process of learning to read an alphabetically based written language necessitate for most children, at the least, an acquaintance with the decoding system by which letters and words mirror, in their bizarre and irregular manner, the sound system of the spoken language.

Here some kind of phonics instruction seems both rational and necessary. It just doesn't happen by itself for the large majority of five-, six-, and seven-year-olds. But there is another developmental complication. The whole language advocates make much of the fact that their views are built out of our scientific knowledge of the reading process. They invoke the meaning orientedness of psycholinguistics.

According to the theory of psycholinguistics, true reading is encoding meaning directly from printed matter and *not* just breaking the word down to its spoken sound equivalent. In order to do this, a child must be able to read featurally, that is, to distinguish the bits and pieces of letters, words, and sentences, at a rate much faster than allowed for by traditional decoding to sound and then to meaning. And while it is true that the mind and developing intelligence of the child are integrating and predicting the information that constitutes meaning, it is the reading system in the child's variable neurology that makes it all possible.

If it were merely a matter of the maturing intelligence of the child, allowing her progressively to be immersed in reading matter and then by some miraculous process, beginning to glean meaning from the printed page, who would object to the claims of whole language advocates? But it doesn't happen often. Children of very high intelligence and maturity often have reading problems, occasionally even being diagnosed as dyslexic. The printed material doesn't always sort itself out in a way that enables the child to internalize it into meaning.

The variability in children's abilities to make the transition to fluent reading—encoding (transmitting) the written material directly into meaning—is great. Children need help from the teacher as well as from the instructional system employed by the school and classroom. To wait for that miracle of transformation that whole language zealots believe will happen as it truly does with the natural spoken tongue is to invite a personal disaster for the unsuspecting and vulnerable child.

The real danger of whole language is that the young child will be abandoned by the school, untaught. Were we discussing an extremely bright, mature ten-year-old fifth grader, with all the literacy skills that we admire, we could take the whole language gamble. Here is a pile of interesting and varied books, magazines, and documents. Sort through them, read what interests you. Then write up some reports, perhaps present orally to the class some of the interesting things that grabbed your attention. Then, read on.

Unfortunately, most of our five- and six-year-olds need much more assistance, teaching, and guidance than that. We have enumerated in the earlier chapters many of the stages that they must of necessity pass through and skills that they must master before they are ready for each step.

In the next chapter, I will discuss the Reading Recovery program which has garnered so much interest in the last few years among practical and concerned teachers. This program starts in first grade and is directed at the seemingly most vulnerable members of each class in reading development. It is literally a crash course of instructional attention and minutely guided one-on-one teaching, making substantial attempts to save children from becoming non-readers—before it is too late.

Many if not most children will need strong phonics assistance in decoding letters and simple words to their sound equivalences. Others, because they are intellectually slower in developing, will need simpler reading materials. These will allow them to decode, even to encode featurally as their reading system matures, all with the goal of comprehension, the enjoyment of the process of reading.

Teachers need to make careful diagnoses of the many varieties of differences that children display. Then, these children deserve and require that the teaching of reading in the classroom be fitted to their particular developmental and learning modalities. Simply, the children will have to analyze words, their sounds, their spelling and component parts.

They will have to be taught how to take words and sentences apart, getting a sense of the spelling differences in the written language as compared with the spoken sounds of the words. In seeing words and sentences taken apart and put back together again, children will be helped to become conscious of the features in the written language and gradually learn to encode those shapes to meaning and then enjoyment.

Whole language advocates either condemn such skill building simply as a deviation from the essence of the teaching of reading process, else they do not account for it at all. Of course, children need to be exposed to and practice the various dimensions of language expression. But each child shows different developmental and talent abilities in the four aspects of language: listening, speaking, reading, and writing. This is because these modalities of language "work off" different parts of the brain and the neurological wiring of its connectors. And each child is unique in this respect.

Further, speech and writing, while both being aspects of one reality—language—are not automatically acquired by human beings in the same way. Indeed, the listened and spoken versions of language are natural and universal. The written and read dimension of language are created, conventional, and learned. They are hardly natural.

Language by eye has taken on many symbolic forms, from the non-sound-linked characters of Chinese logographs to the alphabetic system introduced by the Greeks into Europe. Literacy is hardly universal in human history. Becoming literate therefore requires a completely different set of learning strategies from the spontaneous auditory language immersion that results in a child beginning to understand and then speak.

Here again, with regard to whole language and the literacy panaceas that are now being promoted, exercise extreme caution.

## NOTES

1. Kenneth Goodman. 1986. *What's Whole in Whole Language?* Portsmouth, NH: Heinemann.
2. E. Dechant. 1991. *Understanding and Teaching Reading.* Hillsdale, NJ: L. Erlbaum, 191.
3. J. Chall. 1991. "The New Reading Debates: Evidence from Science, Art, and Ideology." *Reading Teacher* 94(2): 315–327.
4. Dechant, *Understanding*, 169.

# Chapter 10

# *Reading Recovery:*
# *Working at Success*

One doesn't usually think of New Zealand, that sleepy, conservative, English-speaking refuge from the woes of the world, as a fount of educational innovation. Yet in recent decades it has given us two internationally famous educators. Sylvia Ashton-Warner reported on her twenty-year teaching career with Maori children in *Teacher*. Her uniquely human and concrete way of approaching these non-European children in their quest to learn to read and write, and without violating their cultural traditions, made her method a standard for educating the needy as well as the ready, throughout the world.

More recently, Marie Clay has become a name to be reckoned with in literacy education. With long and rich classroom experience, Marie Clay is a more traditional educator than Sylvia Ashton-Warner who, in addition, was a sensitive novelist. Clay has developed an approach, even more than a method, for confronting and dealing with the reality of early reading failure.

This failure, which can become tangible as early as the five-year-old's kindergarten experience and finalized by the close of first grade, when the child is on the threshold of seven years of age, can, if not prevented, close the book on a child's long-term educational future. What Marie Clay's work should represent to us, as it does to the Ohio State University Reading Recovery Institute in Columbus, Ohio, is a quiet but firm refutation of the overblown claims of the whole language advocates for the smooth homogeneous emergent literacy that each child is supposed to achieve when enthusiastically immersed in language.

## BECOMING LITERATE

In Clay's own writings, as derived from her New Zealand experience, the process of becoming literate begins before the child enters kindergarten at five years of age. In the home, the first encounters with the written medium should already have taken place, with, at least, parents reading to the child. Clay's program continues in kindergarten and through first grade.

As developed in the United States, Reading Recovery concentrates on those children identified as being *at risk* early in the first grade, the bottom 10–20 percent of the readers in the first grade. The program bases its actions on long-experienced expectations for reading progress. Such children are taken from the class for thirty minutes per day for a ten- to fifteen-week period and given intensive instruction and guidance in the readiness, mediated, and normal reading skills that first graders are expected to attain.

Marie Clay, having, in addition to the traditional European children, experienced the special problems of youngsters of Maori background, knows full well that teachers and parents should not assume any prior print knowledge when beginning to expose children to the world of reading and writing.

Thus, the basic left-to-right movements of eye, finger, and voice must be pointed out to many preschool and elementary-age children. It is a reality, in addition, that many children in kindergarten and first grade must be taught the difference in appearance between a book right side up and upside-down. Better that these kinds of experiences begin at home, even to the point of showing one's own child the spaces between letters, words, and paragraphs, and explaining why these differences exist and the function they serve.

When we read to the preschooler, translating seemingly meaningless marks on the page into sound, some of the process should be explained, perhaps with the simple example of a letter and its spoken equivalent. The parent need not belabor such relationships. To the child, the fact that such a relationship exists is in itself a miraculous and mysterious reality at first taken for granted, similar to the fact that airplanes can take off from a runway and fly while humans cannot.

The fact that Reading Recovery exists as a massive—in New Zealand, at least—intervention process to rescue children's literacy future from blind fate, ought to make us sensitive to the fact that the path to emerging literacy is often rough and rocky for the child. It is our obligation to intervene pedagogically and apply emergency methods if necessary, to regain the child's rightful developmental place in her classroom.

Marie Clay notes in her writings how often children's relative achievements in reading fluency at the end of the first grade are predictive of where they will stand relative to their peers, three, five, even ten years hence. The tragedy is that the lower and overlooked 20 percent might have had a chance to "recover" and gain grade level stability were some emergency skill and comprehension intervention applied before the frustration of failure dampened the child's will to succeed.

## RECOVERY

It is true that a first-grade teacher will often find that one or several of her students are extremely deficient in their basic print understandings. They may not be able to distinguish a word from a letter, may not have any awareness that spoken words have sound equivalents symbolized in the marks and letters on the page. As Clay puts it, they may not even know the meaning of terms for positions such as first, last, beginning, start, end, and next as they relate to words and sentences.

On occasion, teachers have described situations in which a story was discussed with the children preparatory to having them engage in a lesson of oral reading, including letter/sound identification. When asked to turn to the story, the children would attend not to the writing on the page, rather to the illustrations. The children had not learned earlier that a "story" refers to the written text and not to the illustrations.

**Figure 10.1**
**Beloved Books to Be Shared in School**

The reader may be amazed that such a lack of sophistication exists in our modern world, either in New Zealand or in the United States. Most children can catch on to the print idea quickly, even making the transition from mediated, decoding forms of reading to word and sentence identification with relative ease.

It is important to reiterate, as do those who argue for Reading Recovery, that it is not merely the child of low intelligence who may wind up in the bottom twenty percent of the class. This is why every parent and teacher must follow the simple principle exemplified in Reading Recovery. The individualities of children merely five, six, and seven years of age are too unknown for a teacher to jump to any educational conclusion about their long-term potentialities. We must use every technique in our repertoire to get these children back to the norm of the literacy development expected of their age.

The thirty minutes that the vulnerable child spends with her Reading Recovery teacher are intensive. For the teacher, it is both a diagnostic and pedagogical period. For the child, it is a multidimensional learning experience in various forms of language, reading, and writing skill building, as well as comprehension deepening. In all of this, the teacher attempts to develop the child's print mastery without bringing these various skill attainments to the consciousness of the child, that is, the teacher does not over-verbalize them.

The reason for this has been discussed earlier in this book: Reading involves a process of automatic "featural" perceptions that are integrated into our understanding. We don't want to interfere with what Clay calls *automaticity* in developing fluency in reading. This was the problem with systematic rule-oriented phonics instruction. Children had to apply so many rules that their short-term memory often broke down, and they forgot what they had read previously. Thus, comprehension failed.

The word *monitoring* is often used in Reading Recovery in-service teacher training programs. It is used to alert the teacher to the fact that each child must be guided away from the Reading Recovery program—with its heavy emphasis on teacher-student interactions and instruction—to the time when she will gradually become an independent reader. The subtitle of Marie Clay's most recent book is "The Construction of Inner Control." In other words, eventually, all the skills the teacher has introduced to the child must be absorbed and digested as part of her individual inner repertoire of skills, to be invoked instantaneously and spontaneously as she reads.

Monitoring means that with each developing phase of the intensive Reading Recovery program, the child must be alerted to her own discovery of possible errors that she might make. One of the most common errors takes place when a child reads a sentence and makes a miscue. Thus, in the sentence, "the monkey ate the coconuts," the child might substitute the word "banana" for "coconuts," perhaps having seen a banana as part of the illustration for this story about animals.

The teacher would not necessarily tell the child that correct word, rather ask the child to look again at the sentence and read it once more, and might even suggest that she sound out the word in question. The teacher might point to the word, so that the child herself would recognize the error she made by not attending visually to all the written material.

At the first-grade stage in reading, most children have spoken vocabularies, and the accompanying understanding, that go far beyond their current reading and writing abilities. Thus their minds often speed ahead of their developed reading systems and they invent an appropriate, but incorrect, word—a miscue.

## THE PROGRAM

### Concrete Caring

The thirty minutes a day of "one-on-one" instruction for ten to fifteen weeks that is provided to troubled early readers in the Reading Recovery program represents a crucial illumination of awareness for the teaching profession. It is a bright red light that alerts teachers and school to resolve: We will not allow one single additional day to pass that permits this child to slip unnoticed into the next grade. We refuse to pass the problem on to the next grade teacher, who presumably will only pass the deficiency on once again, until the child slips into adolescent failure.

Such malfeasance would be unintentional on the part of the teachers. Certainly, the defect would be with the school and its program. The child, young and unaware, would never know what was occurring, for she is dependent upon the wisdom, responsibility, and compassion of teacher and school to attend to her needs. But such a result is the fear of all parents and true educators.

Using the latest fad as a crutch, many teachers (and this includes "whole language" enthusiasts) cling to the idea of a great utopian method, preferring an abstraction to the complex and obscure realities of the individual and vulnerable child. They blindly accept every new method that comes along, unthinkingly hopping from one fad to the next. What every child really needs is the teacher's concrete and undivided attention.

This is not a new message. We learned the same lesson after a punishing decline in American industry in the 1970s. Products came off the assembly lines that never should have been accepted. A big red light should have flashed here, too, and the line immediately shut down until everything was "made right," for it was not until the late 1980s and 1990s, and only after great struggle, that industry righted itself. By this time, much had been permanently lost.

In the same manner, Reading Recovery attends to that critical concern, that no child be allowed to slip down during a bureaucratic passing of the buck. It is interesting to note that schools that have instituted Reading Recovery in first grade do not even allow for or pass the child through because of the fact that a weak reader might be quite young, not even six before she enters the first grade in September. The child is still noticed and the wheels of recovery and normalization are set in motion immediately.

### Roaming

What do Reading Recovery teachers do? The answer, for many veteran observers, is that they do not do much more, nor could they be expected to do much more, than old-time teachers did in their first-grade classrooms, before the convenient crutch of educational jargon and ideological rhetoric allowed many teachers to relieve themselves of tedious but crucial day-by-day, minute-by-minute reading instruction. Yet today they might have every available tool in their instructional repertoire ready to fly to the aid of the child. Simply, we do not know what will work, because for 90 percent of the first graders who are at risk, we cannot be sure what the problem is.

The goal in all first-grade programs is to lead the child on an ever-ascending arc of word and sentence recognition. The fact that this may not be happening at the rate and fluency that one expects from first graders requires intervention.

*Roaming* describes the period of the first two weeks with the at-risk child during which a series of informal diagnostic tests is carried out to find out where the beginning of the child's problem is. The problem could be very basic, as in the child's not being aware of the alphabetic principle that written symbols, letters, and words are reflected in the spoken language.

Such levels of awareness are usually achieved in preschool or kindergarten, if not before. If this were not the case, the child might not be able to see or distinguish distinct letter differences. Therefore, the actual recovery program would consist of an intensive process of sensitizing the child to the distinct sound of the spoken language.

Much attention to identifying letters as beginning-, middle-, end-of-the-word elements will be necessary, rather than simply displaying an "a" or "m," as illustrated in a book, on a wall poster, or on a felt board. This kind of skill building would at the same time necessitate practice in correlating the sounds of words spoken or illustrated in books with the actual written versions, that is, phonics.


## Skill Building

If skill building is practical and concrete, and not infused with rule memorizing, it should not be objectionable. Whole language advocates see skill building as dirty words. However, for many children, the road to fluent reading is built out of much preparatory readiness and mediated reading instruction.

If children can be brought to the stage of hearing the distinct sounds of their speech, becoming conscious of these sounds in the sense of being able to *hear* the differences between "*m*ommy" and "*n*onny" or "*z*ebra" and "*ch*eetah," it will likely become possible for them to recognize the functional differences between, "z," "c," "ch," "k," in various written words.

It will even be necessary for some children to trace, manually, the letters on the felt board or in the book, or for the teacher to show them how to write these letters, if their small muscle skills are up to it. All such activities will ready the children to observe and understand the purpose of the differences between letters, and then words.

Often, the difficulty in these young problem readers lies in their slow rates of reading, which often lead to short-term memory breakdowns and a loss of comprehension by the time they reach the end of the sentence. The reasons are many, one being the possibility of slow intellectual development. Comprehension and the search for meaning are at the heart of the reading process. Thus the eyes and *reading system* of the child are often pulled through the text by her inquiring mind.

Sometimes it is simply lack of practice in the regular classroom. Children do need immersion in reading materials, but they also need a teacher who will guide them to decode difficult words or show them how to move their eyes along the page with a pushing finger, even to set a time limit to read an easy passage silently before the book gets closed and the questions are asked and the discussion begun.

Reading Recovery as a technique focuses essentially on the word, identifying it as a unit—the old look-say—or sounding it out, thence to see it as a whole, finally being able to move rapidly through the sentence to accomplish comprehension and pleasure. The techniques for facilitating this goal are myriad at this state—whatever does the trick, using a piece of cardboard to help the child's eye from wandering below the line, sometimes isolating words, pointing to one at a time.

### Few Failures

Care must be taken to make sure that the child does not guess the words solely from the context or the picture. She should be using enough print clues to avoid meaning miscues. It all involves extremely careful teacher guidance, because a clever nonreader, listening to the reading of the other children and using the illustrations as clues, will still over the duration of a first-grade-level story book, miss some words. Then it is the teacher's responsibility to discover what step the child had missed in the delicate process of fluency acquisition, what gaps need to be filled.

Often, as noted above, it is simply the existence of a caring teacher who will say, "Let's look at that word once again and try to read exactly what the writer has put there." The child's response will usually be a less fluent pace of reading. It will often include a greater effort to decode words, awkwardly at first, because heretofore she hasn't had experience or practice in decoding. Yet by keeping the child steadily on track in a book that introduces gradually more complex stories—in vocabulary, content, and sentence structure—the teacher may help strengthen the child's network of neurological connections that later on will create a functioning reading system to work in tandem with her hungry intelligence.

The traditional idea of having children answer questions and enter into discussions with their fellows in reading groups, using both oral and silent reading opportunities, has been a staple of the classroom teachers' responsibilities for many generations of American schooling. Traditionally, every first and second grader had at the least a special half hour put aside for reading group every school day. If a child was struggling, the teacher put aside some time during the day, during recess, lunch, study hours, even after school, to help the child find herself in the reading process.

### Needing a Teacher

Reading Recovery is predicated on the idea that the lower 20 percent that is selected for special help does not constitute a special intellectual or learning disability group. Reading Recovery children do need skill concentrations, and sometimes they even need help reaching an awareness of the meaning function of reading, the idea that books are there to satisfy an interest in knowing about the outside world.

Environmental differences and background can create a needy group. Another intervention-prone group arises from varying intellectual and personality dispositions. These represent children who need an extra learning/guidance push by an attentive and concerned teacher or parent. Other children are slower or different in development, often having modalities of learning, through eye, ear, touch, or emotions, that are out of synch with the given method of the school and classroom.

The Reading Recovery specialist has to be a person who not only has learned efficient techniques of interdiction and failure prevention, but also must be a broad and nondogmatic human being. So often the children in question will be truly different in terms of fitting the model of those whom the Reading Recovery program was designed to help. At that moment the potentiality of a teacher's flexible mind and an open heart can become this struggling child's salvation.

**Figure 10.2**
**A Young Author and His Editor**

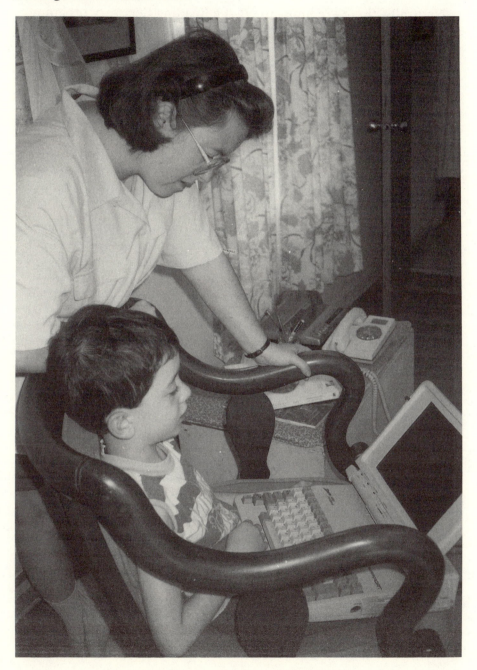

## WHAT CAN READING RECOVERY ACCOMPLISH?

Naturally, there are limits to what a Reading Recovery program, as presently structured in the first grade, can achieve in turning incipiently failing readers into total come-from-behind winners. Let us first emphasize once again the contributions of this reading approach.

First grade, or the period between six and seven years, is crucial in the reading and literacy sequence. By age seven, most normal children should have begun to read fluently, that is, be able to translate the letters, words, and sentences of their simple books directly into meaning. This means encoding, not decoding, which is translating the written material into its phonetic or sound equivalents.

That many children have difficulty in making a smooth transition to encoding, or fluent reading, should turn on the caution light in all classroom and home situations. Reading Recovery opens up an institutional pathway, in the maximum of sixteen weeks, thirty minutes per day during which an experienced teacher will first put the child through a careful diagnostic analysis to discover where the difficulties seem to be located.

Often, it will be a simple matter of assisting children in preparing for the natural neurological development of their unique reading system. This is the process during which the teacher helps the child make the transition from decoding to putting words together, learning to recognize letter patterns as they contribute to meaningful units. Letter and word analysis is crucial here as the child becomes subconsciously aware of the purely visual patterns that letters and words make on the road to building sentence meanings and finally transforming all this into stories, wherein the process becomes both comprehensible and fun.

At other times, the Reading Recovery teacher will discover that she must go back to square one. Here the alarm bells in the school and home must ring loudly. For if the child is not aware of the alphabetic principle of sounds—that letters/words are built on a rough equivalency to the spoken word—she may be in trouble. The problem could be extreme environmental deprivation at home and elsewhere, or some educational negligence in kindergarten or preschool, if the child has been previously exposed to such programs.

Or we could be dealing with a child who is slow either developmentally or intellectually. Whatever the case, educational intervention is essential. All children deserve and have a right to a program of studies that meets their unique individual needs.

## How Successful

The important question for parents and educators is the expectation of success. There is an implicit claim for 100 percent normalization by the Reading Recovery advocates. It is important to qualify this claim. For those children whose learning modalities—visual, auditory, or whatever—do not fit the school's existing patterns, Reading Recovery teachers could discover alternate patterns of learning. The best way to reach and teach a young incipient reader is to discover the child's strong modality of learning and emphasize the child's strengths. What we want to do is to help the child to read directly for meaning. Whatever it takes should be done.

There are, however, children who are developmentally behind, who will need more than fifteen or sixteen weeks of attention to move ahead. Other children will have difficulty with reading but do well in other subject areas, showing evidence of good intelligence.

Some of these children may turn out to be clinically diagnosed dyslexics. Such children will have long-term difficulties with reading, as taught and learned in traditional ways. Or these same dyslexic children might outgrow their disability, the origin of which lies in their neurological development. Often they find their own ways to surmount the blockade that nature has put in their way. They quietly discover a wholly unique modality for getting into "deep structure" and meaning.

Reading Recovery programs should at least identify these children, even when they cannot easily turn the long-term reading corner. The worst thing that educators can allow to happen to any child who enters into their care is to allow problems in learning to go unnoticed. Just as bad is the sloughing off of extremely talented children with a shrug of the shoulders and a "they will do all right no matter what!"

Above all, the Reading Recovery program has shown all of us that the myth that all children will learn to read by simple immersion in print, happy stories, and self-chosen curricula is, simply that, a myth. It just isn't so. Experience tells us that the percentage of the God-gifted-few who learn to read with fluency and understanding without close educator guidance and teaching, is extremely small in the United States.

We must understand that the process of learning to read is not a smooth inclined plane. It is a step-like series of maturational events that has many crucial developmental learning transitions, any or all of which could derail the child's upward momentum. That is why careful teacher/parent diagnosis and teaching focus are crucial in understanding where the child finds herself in this learning continuum, and what steps need to be taken to help the child get to the next plateau.

# Chapter 11

# *Writing*

## RELATIONSHIP TO READING

It is universally agreed that to be considered literate one must be able to write as well as to read fluently. Writing and reading both are aspects of language learning. Recall that a prerequisite for writing and reading when we first enter the human circle is the ability to hear as well as speak a language.

When asked what disability an individual might feel to be more disastrous for our functioning as a human, deafness or blindness, most individuals would agree that deafness would be the more tragic affliction of the two. It separates us from language and thus from the essence of human relations—speech—and then, too, from the abstract forms of literacy, reading and writing. The blind can learn to finger Braille, or listen to "talking books." The deaf must start from behind the line.

Just as children begin to understand language by listening, then speaking, writing is usually thought to be perfected on the heels of previously accomplished reading skills. The language quartet sequence of listening, speaking, reading, and writing are the vehicles by which humans are educated and ultimately gain status as fully civilized and empowered humans.

Writing is different from reading in that it works off different brain skills. One can say that reading is a passive skill for, while the mind is *active* in encoding print into meaning—we put the new reading material into the context of the existing structure of knowledge in our minds—it carries out this process automatically, ordering the new information through the fluent, featural system provided by our reading system.

That is why it is much easier to pick up a book, magazine, or newspaper and read than it is to pick up a pen or pencil and start writing something intelligible on a piece of paper. Likewise with a computer. It is easier to read a message on E-Mail than it is to tap out an intelligible sentence or paragraph and send it out for all the world to see.

Imagine this experiment: Take a group of people with varying reading skills. Analyze these individuals' differences and abilities relative to each other. Then check out their writing abilities. My wager is that the best readers will not necessarily be the best writers. The same for the poorest readers. They might not be at the bottom of the heap in writing ability.

Here are two different systems of language use, reading and writing. Probably (we are still ignorant about the actual structure) they work off different parts of our brain. Thus they are controlled by genetic/developmental factors that are different in each person, just as are the other parts of our physical and mental make-up.

The crux of the relationship between reading and writing is that reading and writing embody two different pathways and expressions on the road to full literacy. They therefore need to be honed and shaped through education with the idea that here, too, individuality has to be sensitively considered. The differences between Sally and Jane in reading are not likely to be similar to their respective differences in writing skills.

## WRITING AND SPEECH

Writing and speaking do have something in common. For one, they require more proactive skill development than the more passive language forms of listening, even reading. As we know, all

**Figure 11.1**
**Diagram of Literacy Development**

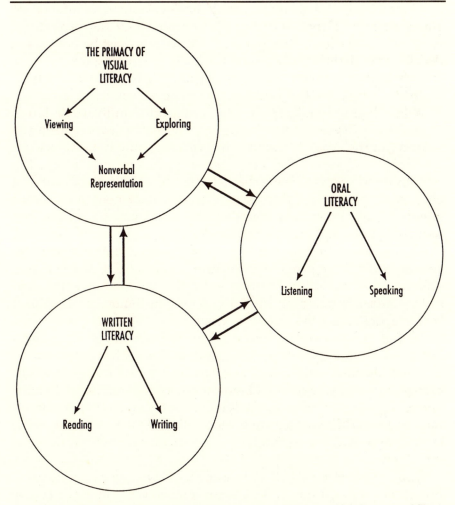

*Source:* From R. Sinatra, *Visual Literacy: Connections to Thinking*, 1986. Courtesy of Charles
C Thomas, Publisher, Springfield, Illinois.

human social groups have developed spoken language. The development of writing by some peoples and not others raises the question as to whether preliterate peoples who have not developed highly sophisticated written grammatical forms have less potential for understanding the more sophisticated versions of the spoken language that come about with literacy.

There is here a rough analogy with the development of infants and young children: They first understand far more than they can express in speech. In a sense, their potential for speech must be honed and developed both through natural exposure to good examples of speech and through conscious teaching. Do they gain in their ability to understand by constantly enlarging their speech skills?

Where highly intelligent but undereducated individuals fail in their literacy development is usually in those two areas, speech and writing. In the case of listening and reading, automatic structures probably exist, especially in the case of understanding speech. The human mind seems to have the natural and universal capacity for constructing language from a natural grammar consisting of the twenty to fifty organizing sounds and phonemes, and syntax—the parts of speech and traditional word order.

As we noted in Chapter 1, young hearing children learn to structure adults' spoken sounds into meaning without self-consciousness or difficulty. The reason for this latent ability has to lie in the preexistence in all humans of certain biological structures that prepare us for the gift of language.

So, too, in the case of reading. The fact that highly intelligent dyslexics cannot learn to read in traditional ways has led scientists to conclude that certain neurological "short circuits" exist in the brains of these individuals. These malfunctions inhibit the spontaneous organization of abstract symbols such as letters and words, making them difficult to be neurologically organized in our reading system and sent on to the deep-structured semantic system, or intelligence.

Remember, however, that reading and writing are secondary human accomplishments. They were achieved only in the last 6,000 years, after a human history of speech that could have originated several million years earlier than that. Writing is thus a later development of civilization rather than a primordial gift from nature. In addition, it requires enormous shaping and diligent practice to become as skilled in writing as in reading. Otherwise, considering the vast number of intelligent people who read on sophisticated levels, we would have many more good writers than we have.

Sensitivity to an awareness of the need to shape the primordial gift of speech is evident in the emphasis placed on it in classical education. Well into secondary and higher education, intense studies were required in speech elocution, grammar, rhetoric, and classical dialectic. These skills were all seen as crucial to the shaping of the educated human.

In fact, and surprisingly, the Greeks generally downgraded reading and writing. These tasks were reserved for scribes and other specialists. The mark of an educated young man in the golden age of Athens was his ability to rise and give a speech to his fellows on some topic of civic importance, or defend a position in the courts of law, being able to think clearly and logically while on his feet before his peers. Would the Greeks have been as aware of the perfectibility of human speech had they not discovered the power of the written medium?

Today, college teachers are aghast when they read student papers. Television and a wide variety of sedentary entertainments have separated students from any awareness of the practical utility, from their self-development as human beings, and from the ability to write clearly and deeply. This concern with writing extends also to speaking, an art lost long ago to "uh, yu-know?" The relationship between the mutual deterioration of speech and writing, the two active linguistic modes, is an important issue that needs study.

Reading fluency, on the other hand, can be attained by the time a child reaches the middle years, fifth and sixth grade. By this we mean that the actual instruction and day-by-day checking—to see whether students are penetrating the deeper conceptual levels of various reading assignments, both fiction and fact—should be completed as youngsters move into subject matter learning.

The job of teaching writing at the higher skill levels, however, continues long into young maturity. This can and should be said of the teaching of speech. Both need steady and continuing perfection by practice and criticism well into the mature years.

## WRITING HELPS READING

To help us understand the relationship of writing to reading, it may be useful to recall the special service of language for human beings. It is probably unique to our species to be able to use sound in producing not merely a call system of communication—what chimpanzees, dogs, and dolphins use to communicate their feelings. Humans also utilize a system of sounds that are symbols of meaning, often representing objective statements about how the world works. We can do this because our vocal system is linked to a complex and neurologically rich brain structure.

Language is a specialization unique to humans in comparison to animals. But it is nothing unless it is linked to our intelligent brain. Test it out when you attend mass celebrations, political meetings, rock concerts, or sports events: there is much sound, expostulation, emotional sloganeering, but not much meaning. Language can take us down as well as up. It depends on how we use it.

The purpose of both reading and writing is to create meaning. I say "create" even in the process of reading. For, while our reading system helps to translate the written symbols into a featural structure of shapes that the mind can translate into meaning, and does so for many children with amazing speed and ease, it is yet a process of "meaning creation."

That is why educators react so indignantly to the hours of television-watching in which children engage. Here the mind plays a far more passive role, ingesting the visual images and carrying forward little mental content or depth of understanding. Understanding, to be useful, must at some moment in a person's future be capable, as with print, of being related to other structures of meaning. The visual mind operates differently from the literate mind, with much less power, long-term memory, and conceptual fall-out.

Both reading and writing demand the full utilization of one's intellect. When you write, even a brief poem, you attempt to create meaning. To do so, you have to probe the deep-structure understanding of relationships, ideas, and facts. All this must be put together into a whole, a composition, a letter, a report. It is an activity that literally regenerates the brain cells.

In theory, every human being has only one deep-structured understanding. We mine and advance this understanding in many ways. That is why concerned parents see the necessity to give their children music lessons, extra physical education opportunities, and expose them to travel, museums, and concerts. All these enrich and advance their children's inner powers.

**Figure 11.2**
**Writing and Drawing: Creative, with Orthodox Spelling**

I got to play nintendo evry day
they had Fo and
strctfi'dr and fout ball
and basball to.

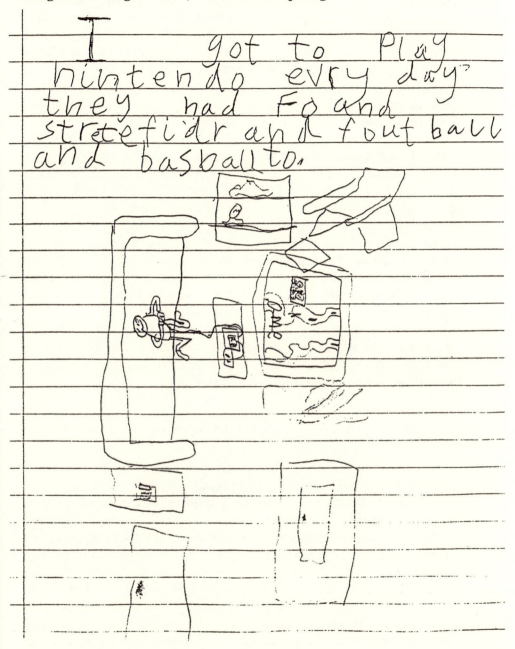

So, too, writing confronts the language problem directly. The child gives back through the piece of paper some of the understandings that she has gleaned through the reading process. In creating meaning through writing, the child becomes more familiar with what is, for example, in musical notation and mathematical symbols, an abstract structure of meaning. Writing practice allows the print medium to become increasingly "user-friendly."

Just as learning a foreign language is seen as internalized and natural by the time one begins to dream in the language of the foreign tongue, so, too, constant immersion in the written form of language, through either reading or writing, but especially the latter, brings the child that much closer to achieving literacy. One writes what one thinks. Even the interpretation through reading a great novel cannot reproduce the intimacy of print that a youngster achieves in composing and writing a simple letter.

The rule is that the various modalities of language as we use them reinforce each other, because they all use language to create meaning. Thus children are led into the vast internality of their minds-in-the-making. Children define themselves through what they think, understand, and mentally crave. Writing gives to children the power to reveal this self-defining innerness as it is shaped by use. It cannot help but to unlock in some mysterious way the meanings that others are attempting to communicate in their own writings. This the child will discover through reading, and smile with pleasure and recognition as she does so.

## SPELLING: INVENTED AND ORTHODOX

Spelling is called a surface-structure skill. It is an aspect of that intermediate zone that we call the reading system. Because of the variability that individuals exhibit in spelling, and because spelling exists on the interface between what we hear and how we write the sounds of our language, it is probable that spelling ability or disability relates little to our perceptual sensitivities, to our hearing and seeing.

Also, it is clear—and all parents should be well-informed of this fact—that spelling skills have little relationship to an individual's intellectual, reading, or writing abilities. That is why we call it a "surface" skill. It does not touch on the deep-structured intellectual thinking capacities of the individual. It is similar to handwriting.

It has been close to a century since anyone tried to relate the beauty or ugliness of handwriting to one's ability to think, reason, or express something reasonably fluently in writing.

Before the word processor and the many valuable programs for checking spelling through the computer, there was a value in being able to spell: to communicate with the outside world. Perhaps one could argue that a minimal level of literacy and education would be symbolized by writing that adhered to the given orthodox spelling traditions of our literary heritage. Today, even with the "spelling checker" in the word processor, we still have to come fairly close to the orthodox spelling of a word, or the program will state on the screen, "no alternates."

In the traditional classroom, spelling was an established part of the language arts program. We had spelling workbooks, weekly spelling tests, and spelling bees. Ultimately, the best spellers went to the "nationals," perhaps to make the local school famous. It was always a wonder why some children had this almost photographic memory or sense of the correctness of a word's spelling, for surely the English language is damnably irregular and tricky. Other children in the class, seemingly just as bright in so many subject areas, including reading, would produce a page of written work that would be literally smeared with red marks.

Even before the controversy over "invented spelling" arose, the issue of spelling drills and competency was beginning to fade under the light of the realization that spelling skills told us little about the literacy of individuals.

"Invented spelling," which will be described below, brings back memories of the controversies over an earlier spelling innovation. This was ITA, the Initial Teaching Alphabet. ITA was argued for back in the 1960s as a revolutionary method to allow youngsters in preschool, kindergarten, and the first two grades to learn to read phonetically, without the usual complexities of phonic rules memorization or the problem of making the transition to fluent reading.

ITA, as discussed earlier in Chapter 5, established forty-four letter/combination symbols (graphemes) that mirrored the forty-four phonemes, or basic sounds of CBS (Columbia Broadcasting System), that is, orthodox spoken English. Once the children learned to relate these forty-four symbols to their spoken language sounds, they could write in ITA every thought that came into their minds, without any spelling "errors." Everything was "regular" in

ITA. No exceptions, nor dozens of rules to be learned, later un-learned. Eventually a smooth transition would be made to TO (traditional orthography).

This transition usually took place during the end of first or the beginning of second grade when the children are beginning to be able to read fluently. A good ITA reader had no problem in making the transition, for the inventor of the method, Sir James Pitman, had taken pains to insure that the upper parts of the ITA letters were the same as the upper parts of the TO letters. Children beginning to read fluently and with the full empowerment of their "reading system" neurology could make the transition seamlessly.

The problem of transition lay in the areas of writing and spelling. Many youngsters had to relearn their spelling. Spelling was so easy and regular in ITA, whereas spelling in the orthodox TO (traditional orthography) was frustratingly irregular. Nonetheless, the transition was duly accomplished by the vast majority of children. The reason ITA failed to take hold universally was that more and more preschoolers came to school with a knowledge of TO and were already able to write "cat," not "kat," for example. The redundancy of teaching two alphabets, and the costs of materials and training teachers, gradually withered the movement and ITA disappeared.

"Invented spelling" has the same goal as ITA—to enable children to write without the tedious corrections and copying that they would have to undergo were they taught to write exclusively by the "correct" spelling approach. The ideal is that as children begin to learn to read, as their small motor coordination improves enough to write clearly, and often well before they can write on a straight line, they should be able to express their ideas and thoughts in writing, without having to wait until they are old enough to absorb the do's and dont's of orthodox spelling.

In the early 1970s, Charles Read published a series of studies on the development of children's writing. He established five stages in their developmental awareness of the "alphabetic principle":

1. Pre-Communicative Stage. Here children scribble their sense of what might stand for letters. It is rare for children of age three or four to do more than draw approximate lines and curves, sometimes left to right, sometimes up and down. Infrequently, under the special

stimulus of a parent or preschool teacher, the child will be able to repeat shapes that represent specific sounds or letters.

2. Semi-Phonetic Spelling. Children begin to represent some of the spoken phonemes of words as letters, using them consistently with the same words. In this they show that they have caught on to the alphabetic principle of our language. Examples of this stage would be "et" for "eat," "clx" for "close," "gls" for "girls." Around the age of five, children begin to reflect this awareness in their writing.

3. Phonetic Spelling. Gradually children advance in their awareness of the alphabetic principle, realizing that each sound of the spoken language has a special letter equivalent. Children begin to hear and demonstrate in writing the difference between consonants and vowels, and are even able to discern the difference between short and long vowels, present and past tenses. Examples: "dras" for "dress," "pekt" for "peeked," "bat" for "bat," "bet" for "bait," or "I hep uou lek tas pacherr" for "I hope you like this picture." This stage is ordinarily achieved at around six-and-a-half years of age.

4. Transitional Spelling. Children at this stage are on the road to orthodox spelling. They have begun to internalize the rules and patterns of English spelling, including vowels, in all their writing. They continue to resolve difficult words with their own phonetic interpretations, as with "eagel" for "eagle," "highcked" for "hiked," "mene rascule" for "mean rascal." But they are now more amenable and ready to correct for the standard spelling. This stage should be under way by the time children have passed their seventh birthday.

5. Conventional Spelling. At this point in children's educational development, usually after seven-and-a-half years of age, or in the latter half of the second grade, children should have within their spelling memory a repertoire of common and easy words. Naturally, depending on their surface-structure skills in this area, they may misspell new words.

Some children will remain poor spellers, retaining little of what they see and read, often even write, in consistently irregular spelling patterns. These children may be brilliant readers, seldom even noticing the actual letters and words that they read. They read directly for meaning, needing few visual features to organize into meaning even fairly difficult new reading materials. Not only are they bright intellectually, but they have well-functioning reading systems except for the spelling dimension.

**Figure 11.3**
**Print: Traditional Spelling**

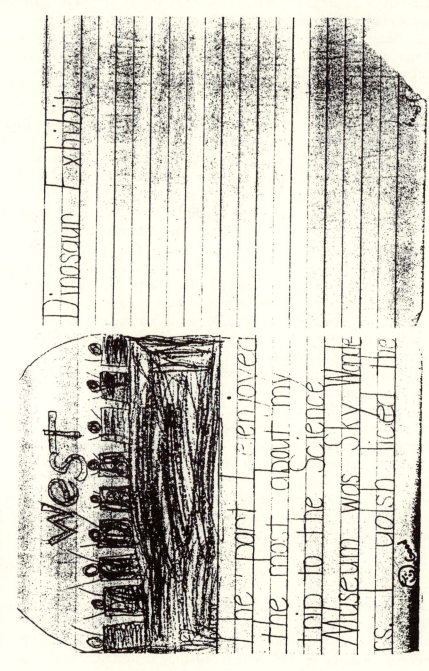

*Source: Reading to Learn in the Content Areas* by Judy S. Richardson and Raymond F. Morgan, copyright © 1994 by Wadsworth, Inc. Reprinted by permission of the publisher.

**Figure 11.4**
**Invented Spelling: Stages**

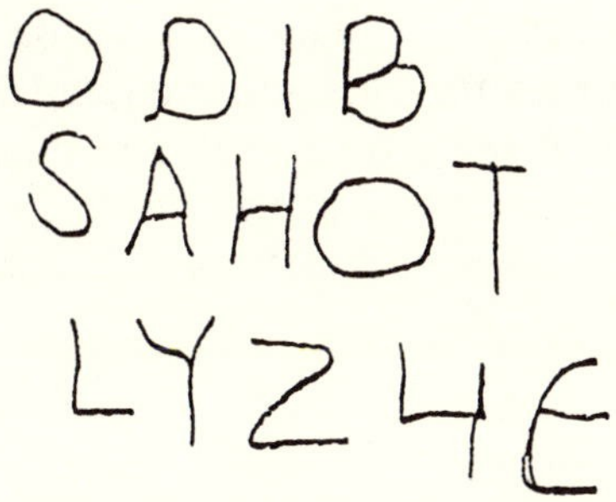

O DIB
SAHOT
LYZ4E

Pre-phonemic: Age 4

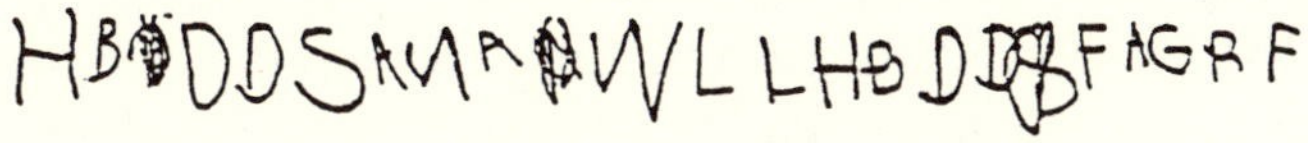

HB DDDSAMA WL LHD DFAGRF

Early phonemic: Kindergarten (age 5–6), A Nursery Rhyme

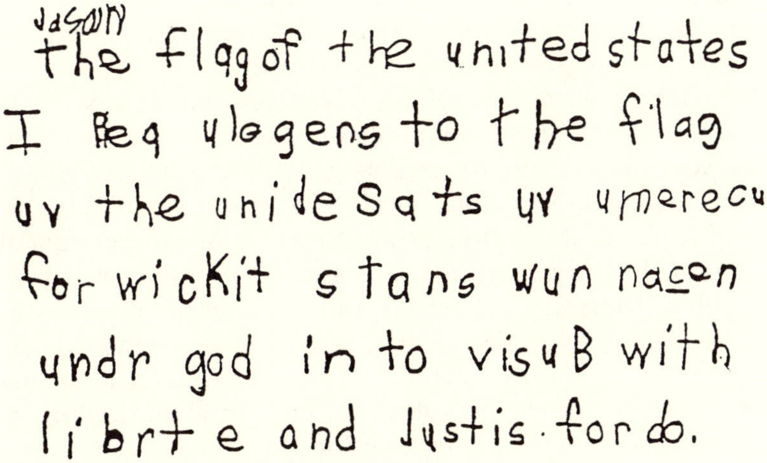

Jason
the flag of the united states
I feq ulegens to the flag
uv the unide Sats uv umerecu
for wickit stans wun nacen
undr god in to visuB with
librte and Justis for do.

First grade (age 6–7), Pledge of Allegiance

143

This should forewarn us against jumping to conclusions too rapidly about a child's potential on the basis of such early learned skills. Writing, and the spelling dimension, are separable from reading in terms of success and failure. They derive from neurological systems in the brain that are independently variable from one child to the next. Too often our lack of awareness of these developmental differences in learning causes us to fall back on easy but dangerously global cause-and-effect conclusions about children.

## CONTROVERSY

In the "good old days," children would copy short sentences from a workbook using the spaces below the sentences, sometimes helped by dotted outlines, sometimes not. Whether such writing experiences began in kindergarten or in first grade, the idea was to initiate the child gradually into orthodox spelling.

When the child attempted to write a creative story, a sentence or two, the teacher would often help the child with the syntax, word order, and spelling. The important thing was that the child, as she began to learn to write, mirror the spelling of the words that she was simultaneously reading.

The advocates of "invented spelling" have a different perspective on the matter. Their view is that the child must be immersed in the experiences of all the language modalities. Since the act of writing reflects a process in which the inner language of thought or of speech is expressed in outward form, it is essential to smooth the way for the meaning-creating act that writing is.

Further, many invented spelling advocates oppose any imposition of orthodox spelling disciplines on the child, for they might interfere with the productive language act. They believe that the obstacles created by requiring formalistic surface-structure rules could be hurtful to the child's desire to write. As one reading and writing authority phrases it," teachers should deemphasize conventional spelling during this period and be tolerant of children's invented spelling, even celebrating students' nonstandard spellings. By analyzing spelling errors, teachers can determine when children have reached the fifth stage [of] conventional spelling, and are ready for formal spelling instruction."[1]

The question that parents often raise to such a rationalization for invented spelling is whether the child will ever reach the conventional spelling stage if her spelling is not corrected as she is maturing into that developmental level. Since we are discussing the evolution of a child's ability to master the alphabetic principle and thereby translate the sounds of speech into a consistent and regular written code, it is critical to show the child the conventions of this very necessary code. Should we promote the momentary written urges of the child, and her momentary inventions of spelling, which often vary from one minute to the next? If we do so, will the child be able to translate and read what she wrote five minutes earlier?

Much of the rationale behind invented spelling has its origins in the whole language movement's need to see every child engaged creatively in all the language modalities. However, such whole language/invented spelling arguments do raise questions about the nature of the creative urges of children between five and seven years of age. One response is that creativity is not a homogeneous "thing." Five- and six-year-olds have different creative needs from those of a mature Virginia Woolf or William Faulkner.

Do we really deprive children of selfhood by showing them the correct spelling of the word "Spot" or "with" when they are trying to write "My dog Spot is fun to play with"? In fact, one could argue that the interaction between the orthodox spelling that the child is learning to read and the creative stories that she is trying to write needs to be reinforced through the orthodox spelling.

Naturally no modern teacher would penalize or reprimand youngsters of five-, six-, or seven-years-of-age for making spelling errors in a story. But why is it educationally wrong-headed to begin to show them how the spelling system of the written language works so that they can show their stories to their parents and friends, and even have others read what they have written?

Invented spelling carried to extremes by dogmatic whole language advocates would impose unnecessary handicaps on children's normal desires to obtain mastery over a new medium—writing—just when children are beginning to perceive its communicative power. In the long run, the key to releasing an individual's creativity is not merely to indulge the desire to express one's ideas and imagination, but to be able to communicate those ideas to others. Further, it is important that children be able to read these ideas immediately after they have written them.

Finally, if we are concerned about children's opportunity to express creative ideas and thought, the oral medium is a wonderful modality at this age level. Children love to tell stories, both making them up and repeating what they have heard. The thinking and speaking are there, only the still-maturing written skills are not utilized. But they can be, and the children will gain the added pleasure of seeing their creative powers enhanced with the skills of almost correct writing and spelling.

## COMPUTERS?

The quick reply to the implied question is a resounding "yes!" As soon as children gain some experience with the alphabetic principle and its relationship to writing and reading, they are ready to use a computer or word processor to tap out their thoughts. The problem with using the computer—the actual mechanics of working it—should provide no problem to a six-year-old.

Young children find handwriting in capital letters easier than upper-and-lower-case printing or in cursive. Primarily this is because the small motor controls of five- or six-year-olds are not yet well developed. Thus, children are taught to write first in block letters.

These problems are neatly avoided through the use of computers. Even the controversy over invented spelling is rendered moot. Children are immediately presented the actual letters on the keys that they will have to press when writing their stories or reports. Realistically, the computer makes demands on the child that no soft-hearted whole language teacher would dare to make—it imposes either an upper- or lower-case configuration on the alphabet, with no other choices or room for "creativity."

And while a good word processing program should have an excellent spelling checker, the child will still be required to know the approximate spelling of the word so that the phrase "no alternatives" will not appear on the screen. The ability of the computer to override surface-structure differences in penmanship constitutes another real advance for the child on her road toward the freedom to write and correct, both in the actual writing of a story, and also in grammar and syntax.

The computer is quicker and less messy than handwriting. There are no smudged erasures. The computer makes corrections easy, and immediately shows the results of such improvements in surface-structure skills, especially if an inexpensive printer can be part of the computer package. Of course, computers can't do everything yet: spelling checkers are not able to help children with inflectional endings ("they're," "their") or, with homonyms ("piece," "peace").

Still, constant improvements are being made and increasing numbers of word processing programs are designed for children learning to read and write. Every school should have some of these available for in-school use.

## BUILDING SKILLS IN WRITING

Writing involves both surface-structure skills and deep-structure dimensions of meaning. Humans are born with unknown potentialities to think, create, and interact with other humans in a social environment. The purpose of education in any culture is to make those unknown aptitudes manifest so that they work to the best advantage of the growing and maturing child. Writing is one of the four language dimensions that facilitate that development. It is also the most abstract and skill-oriented of the language modalities.

If we know what we want children to achieve through schooling, we can be clear and efficient in going about the task. Children need our rational assistance. In the case of writing, the rule is simple: children need constant practice under the guidance of older or model writers, whether they be parents or teachers.

This means that from first grade and up, the child should be writing and being corrected, helped to be a better communicator, better thinker, and even more efficient creator. Even the most creative poets, novelists, and philosophers endlessly rewrite, correct, tighten, amplify their creative work. Where is the tragedy, then, if we help children to improve by correcting and rewriting? The test is always *how* it is done, psychologically and pedagogically. The worst thing a teacher can do is to let errors go by—not to bother to correct them or show the child how a piece of work could be made tighter, cleaner, or clearer.

It is important to stimulate children to engage in various types of writing. This is because each different piece of writing—poem, fictional story, or encyclopedia report—requires a different mind set, a novel way of approaching the topic. This challenges children to employ different skill strategies to get beneath the surface of their awareness, to mine new language talents. If children aren't asked to think more deeply, they may never become aware of how widely they are able to range.

Naturally, as time goes by and the youngsters are exposed to a broad variety of writing projects, as they constantly rework their writing to squeeze out a reasonable perfection (considering the stage in their development), they themselves will begin to see that their talents reveal that certain language skills are more easily accomplished, and at a higher level. This could be the beginning of a process of awareness of their own talents in one particular area. It might not be in writing at all. It might be in math, music, or art.

The point of education in a civilized setting is to develop the general intellectual power of a person. In the process, we learn about our best skill areas, where we seem to stand a bit beyond the average. This is fair and natural, since otherwise we would not have the richness of talent and experiences that life in advanced societies presents to us. This is the product of the variety of talents that our educational system has inspired.

Literally dozens of different writing projects can be suggested to children in the course of a year, and they can be reworked many times so that the children's feel for the medium is deepened and developed. The issue that causes educational controversy is the creativity versus correction issue, as if there ever were a disjunction here—as if the two goals conflicted. They do not. It is one thing not to give children opportunities to develop their own ideas in written form, and another to believe that all written work springs into creative perfection the first time it issues from the pen or word processor. And there is no reason why reasonable efforts at correcting and improving ought not start in first grade.

In summary, children must be encouraged to mine the dimensions of intelligence and creative power through writing just as they do through the other language modalities. Improvement and empowerment come at the end of a long, complex process of practice, correction, and deepening skill and intellectual awareness. To write well, one must learn to write, rewrite, write again, and again. The substance is there, deep down. Our goal is to help students have the tools to get that substance up and out.

## NOTE

1. Gail E. Tompkins. 1994. *Teaching Writing*, 2d ed. New York: Merrill.

# Chapter 12

# *The School Program*

## GOALS

The purpose of this section is to alert parents and teachers to the broader flags of opportunity as well as dangers in the reading education of each child. Parents need to know the standards of literacy accomplishment for a good school program. How else can they be alerted to problems that may arise at each stage in their child's development? The earlier a parent or a teacher becomes aware that things aren't happening when or as they should, the greater the chance for ultimate intervention and success.

The child passes through three marker stages in the evolution of reading fluency. We have discussed these in earlier chapters, but let us reiterate them and bring these several hurdles together in one place, for parent alertness and for teacher readiness.

## STAGE ONE: ALPHABETIC AWARENESS

From the period of four to six years of age, the child should be exposed to the relationship between the spoken language and its

written form. Writing is built on our ability to speak and understand language. Writing is, however, not dependent on speech.
Many profoundly deaf children learn to read fluently, and then to
write. Also, many children pass almost miraculously from speaking
to distinguishing letters and words. They take a few bare clues from
television or from signs in shopping centers, and begin to read, first
slowly, then fast, fluently, and furiously.

At one time, the percentage of these natural readers, some as
young as age five, was higher than it is today. For the great majority
of children today, the transition from the naturalness of speech to
the artificiality of reading and writing will have to come about as
the result of systematic instruction.

That is the important point for parents. Parents, be concerned
about school programs wherever you hear this message: "Your child
will learn to read naturally by immersing herself in books." Both
child and parent may discover two or three years later that the
expected reading accomplishment didn't happen and it may well
be too late for easy remediation.

Your child needs steady guidance and supervision to make the
transition from an awareness of the sounds of the spoken language
to the printed alphabetic representation of the sounds, as unsys-
tematic a relationship as that might be. Following that, she needs
guidance to put these sound-letter equivalents into words. Either
she will need to learn to sound out words through a mediated (let
us hope nondogmatic) phonics program, or by sight recognition
teaching.

The key issues are teaching, classroom observation and diagnosis
of problems, and an awareness by the school that the process
should reach a climactic stage of readiness, or emergence, or
however one wishes to phrase it, sometime in grade one. If the
child is not decoding words to sound by mid-first grade, and with
some speed, the bells should go off.


## STAGE TWO: FLUENCY

During this stage, parent and teacher both should be carefully
observing the transition of the child to fluent reading. There is an
overlap here with Stage One. In general, children between the ages
of five and seven (between kindergarten and second grade) go
through this stage.

**Figure 12.1**
**The New England Primer**

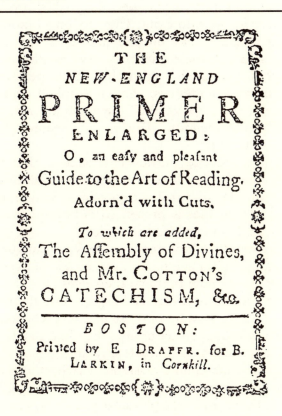

THE
*NEW-ENGLAND*
PRIMER
ENLARGED:
O, an easy and pleasant
Guide to the Art of Reading.
Adorn'd with Cuts.

*To which are added,*
The Assembly of Divines,
and Mr. COTTON'S
CATECHISM, &c.

*BOSTON:*
Printed by E DRAPER. for B.
LARKIN, in *Cornhill.*

In Adam's Fall
We sinned all.

Thy Life to mend,
This Book attend.

The Cat doth play,
And after slay.

A Dog will bite
A Thief at Night.

An Eagle' flight
Is out of sight.

The idle Fool
Is whipt at School

As runs the Glass,
Man's life doth pass.

My Book and Heart
Shall never part.

Job feels the rod,
Yet blesses God.

Kings should be good
No men of blood.

The Lion bold
The Lamb doth hold

The Moon gives light
In time of night.

What we want children to achieve by the end of second grade is the maturation of the child's reading system. This means that instead of sounding out words—decoding—they are beginning to read too rapidly for sounding out. They no longer mouth the words with their lips, rather they encode the visual marks directly to meaning. This doesn't mean that they have to read especially fast. The key is that by visually skimming the upper surface of the letters, words, and sentences, they are able to translate these marks—through the logic of their own unique neurological systems—directly into meaning. During this second stage, reading should begin to be fun.

Some whole language enthusiasts believe that this process should happen naturally. They immerse the children in literature. This can be a wonderful learning experience. Sometimes, however, the reading material that is presented is beyond the child's skill development, and many a child flounders.

Skill development is a taboo concept to whole language devotees, but most children will have to gain some ease of decoding. A few must even be taught how to move their eyes over the page before they can ever hope to begin to read rapidly and fluently.

Parents, I reiterate: Beware of those teachers who assure you that fluent reading will happen naturally. The child needs to be taught and guided. You should not tolerate any abnegation of educational responsibility in your child's classroom! If by the second half of second grade your child is having difficulties in reading fluently with good comprehension and deep pleasure, you must spring into action.

There are three warning signs to look for: (1) Lack of awareness of some of the basic alphabetic principles of the written language—directionality of print on the page; the sound system embedded in the written symbols; or that print communicates meaning and ideas. These are all basics that the child should have picked up in kindergarten or early first grade. Without such awareness a child could be in serious difficulty.

(2) Slow and halting decoding of the written symbols to sound. Often this child cannot remember the beginning words of the sentence by the time the last word is sounded out. Also, there may be reversals of letters in oral reading, sentence confusions, beginning and ending mix-ups.

If any of the above characteristics are associated with chaotic writing, with reversals, or with incoherent spatial relationships in writing words and short sentences, your child may be exhibiting dyslexic symptoms. Specialized diagnostics are immediately war-ranted. The school should help in such circumstances. If not, the parent should take the initiative and get the child to a reading clinic, which is often associated with a university or college. Many medical centers have facilities for the diagnosis of neurological handicaps, which are often the source of dyslexic symptoms.

(3) Slow reading and low comprehension. Your child is able to decode words into their sound equivalents, and is sometimes even able to identify words without sounding them out. But the reading is slow and the comprehension—this includes making sense out of the reading, answering questions about it, and summarizing its contents in oral or written form—is often fuzzy. The child may be slow intellectually or developmentally. In either case, special concern must translate itself into a program whereby the child is neither ignored by the teacher nor ostracized by the other children in the class.

A strategy must be planned to give this child the careful, kind, and steady assistance to develop her literacy skills. A few more years into elementary schooling and the child could surprise everyone by shooting forward in subject matter mastery, if not in reading and writing. Each human being is different. The crime lies in making too many quick and early assumptions and decisions concerning a child's long-term future.

In summary, we have worldwide guidelines today as to the developmental rates of reading progress. Therefore, no child should be allowed to slip through this sequence of educational expecta-tions of progress merely through the ignorance of the educational authorities. It is a myth to believe that, on their own, all children will succeed equally and easily in becoming fluent and compre-hending readers.

Parents must immediately investigate if by the end of second grade their child is not on the road toward reading fluency. We can afford to be approximate in our expectations of the developmental reading progress of each child from the ages of three through seven. However, toward the end of this time sequence, as we will note later in this chapter, the great separation begins to take place between purely developmental differences in children and their long-term intellectual achievements.

It is essential that each child be carefully monitored by all concerned before the age of eight as to the whys and wherefores of their reading development. Second grade, or age seven-and-a-half, is the boundary point of reading maturation. Parents should never allow their child to pass beyond this point without being sure of her progress, prognostics, and the in-place educational plan ready to deal with any diagnosed problems.

## STAGE THREE: COMPREHENSION

By third grade, the spread between children's levels of reading competency begins to widen. No longer are the purely developmental factors, as between the precocious early reader and the intelligent late-bloomer, crucial. By third grade, the bright late fluent readers have caught up with the bright early readers. In general, by the time children are in third grade, we can usually begin to define their general academic potential, especially their reading abilities.

In fourth grade, important and predictive achievement tests, sponsored by the federal government and the state, will begin. All the various subject matter skills, including arithmetic, will be tested. Each year that passes with a child continuing to fall behind in basic skills will affect her general educational and vocational future. This is not a happy fact to report.

This reality serves to underline the enormous responsibility of the classroom teacher to see to it that all the children within the class are being exposed to, and instructed in, a wide variety of thinking skills as they involve comprehension.

Some children fly through all sorts of problem solving activities, from map reading to math verbal problems. Others, with just as powerful intellectual potentialities, but less overt performance skills, need more guidance and day-by-day monitoring before they can break loose and start to fly on their own. Something clicks in their minds, often because an insistent teacher or parent did not let them slide away from confronting and trying to learn the entire repertoire of reading and thinking tasks and subject matters.

A teacher or parent has literally dozens of reading and writing challenges with which to stimulate a child in both the daily instructional sequence of learning and over a period of weeks and months of steady teaching, evaluation, practice, monitoring, and correcting. What follows represents only a few of the different kinds of day-to-day experiences for thought and analysis that a reputable language program, which would include both reading and writing, should have. All these activities require much careful record keeping and constant follow-up within the school year. For the child, it should be hard work, but it should also be fun, like a challenging game.

Finding main ideas in paragraphs; developing standards for evaluating and critiquing a story or book the child reads; discovering synonyms and antonyms for interesting words; substituting different colorful words in a story for variety; becoming competent in the use of maps, dictionaries and encyclopedias, time-tables, and graphs; understanding and interpreting a variety of graphic illustrations of data; being able to write a short summary of a longer article including the important data; writing a short sentence about a longer piece of fiction or nonfiction stating the main idea; trying one's hand at reading and writing poetic forms; writing an imaginative story; reading math problems for conceptual as well as calculative understanding—crucial with the use of calculators; learning to read actual experimental problems, and thus understanding the vocabulary and meaning of scientific method—problem, hypothesis, prediction, test, data, conclusion, confirmation, and error; reading to discover new words and their relationship with old words; taking main idea notes from oral dictation; learning to read quickly—in a testing situation—so as to answer questions sequentially placed before the reading material; outlining the structure of a chapter in a social studies text for levels of importance of facts and interpretation.

The key teacher responsibility is to maintain the reading/language program for each child on three simultaneous levels of instruction:

1. The independent level. Here the child is confident and competent to read and learn on her own.

2. The instructional level. This represents the boundary of the child's abilities, where the teacher is an all-important support, always ready with an idea for developing a useful or timely skill, ever turning new learning into great successes.

3. The frustration level. At this level, the teacher periodically, more often than rarely, puts the child through her paces with material that is seemingly beyond her chronological and instructional levels, material far in advance of her abilities.

Sometimes such challenges could involve reading and subject matter difficulties that are as much as two or three grades beyond the present. Such teaching and learning experiments are important because one cannot be sure that the pace of learning in the classroom reflects the child's true ability potential at a particular moment. Children have a way of adjusting to the pace of teaching and learning even when it is below their capacities to advance. Many times teachers present difficult material seemingly beyond the child's current performance, they are startled to find how much was hidden from view.

On the other hand, it is crucial that a teacher back off quickly and gracefully from a failed experiment, presenting the venture as an experiment with material that is "for much older children" rather than implying in any way that the child was a failure. Unfortunately, in an educational environment in which the presumption is that all children" will learn spontaneously and at their own pace," the net result is that students can be educationally neglected, not given the opportunity to press against the often extraordinarily flexible boundaries of their potential.

## DEVELOPMENTAL READING APPROACHES

There is controversy involving pedagogical approaches to teaching reading. Among whole language advocates, the *bête noir* is the basal reader. The basal has been around for many decades, all the way back to McGuffey and before. In the basal series of readers offered by publishers since the 1920s, the goal has been to present stories that children can identify with, while at the same time presenting the children with a graded vocabulary. These were complemented by workbooks and other materials for use in building the various phonic and grammatical skills necessary for subsequent attainments in fluent reading.

Over the years, as the level of reading achievement fell, even among the very young, the basals' vocabularies became increasingly simplistic, as did the stories that were built on these rudimentary vocabularies.

In addition, during the heyday of progressive education and the look-say approach to reading, phonics was much underrated as a tool for building word and sentence fluency. Many children were lost to literacy because of this. Thus, the basals came under attack from the child-centered left as well as the phonics right.

**Figure 12.2**
**McGuffey's** *Eclectic Reader,* **Mid-19th Century**

Today, "basals are beautiful." They touch every possible eclectic base so that they will not incite any stubborn enemies. The stories are interesting, and more and more multicultural. Classics of literature and interesting nonfiction materials are included, and accommodation is sometimes made especially for weak or advanced readers, that is, several parallel versions of a basal may be issued by one publisher.

But because every basal series has a teachers' edition—which includes "teacher-proofed" stereotypical questions to be asked of children about each story, as well as the usual tests and enrichment activities—there has been a understandable cry of grief from the child-centered, language experience or whole language advocates. These latter would prefer a program that emphasizes individualized reading for each child, linked to a rich literature-based program, mostly devoid of drills and so-called "skill building," which they

**Figure 12.3**
**A Geography Lesson for Elementary School Children, 1855**

## LESSON III.

RILLS, BROOKS, RIVERS.

Q. What small streams of water are formed by springs?
A. Rills, Brooks, Rivulets, and Creeks.

Q. What do brooks and rivulets form?
A. They form larger streams of water, called Rivers.

Q. What are the large branches of a river called?
A. They are also called Rivers: small branches, Creeks.

Q. What is the place called, where a river rises or begins?
A. Its source; as, springs on high land, lakes, ponds, etc.

Q. What is the direction in which a river runs called?
A. The direction in which it runs is called its course.

Q. What is the place called where it flows into another body of water?
A. It is called the outlet or mouth of the river.

"He sendeth the springs into the valleys, which run among the hills. They give drink to every beast of the field."

argue interferes with the child's search for meaning and understanding through reading.

Individualized reading programs require of the teacher a diverse set of books and other teaching material for each child. The teacher must program a unique set of readings for each child, and she must file a record of each child's achievements, for communication to the parent as well as the teacher in the next grade.

Individualized reading programs are huge undertakings for any teacher with a class of twenty to twenty-five children. The great task involves the diagnostic individualization of a reading program for each child. This should be accomplished within a reasonable

**Figure 12.4**
**Dick, Jane, and Spot of the 1950s: Controlled Vocabularies, Look-Say Method**

"Look here," said Father.
"Look at Mother and me.
Here we come."

Sally said, "Away we go!
Dick and Jane.
Father and Mother.
Tim and me."

"And Spot and Puff," said Dick.
"Away we go!"

time frame as soon as possible after the beginning of the year. Then the record keeping begins, the necessary correction of the many different written exercises based on the diverse readings. It is a rare mortal educator who can accomplish such a task for more than a year or two without total burnout.

Truly, there is room within any language arts and reading program for a basal reading program. At the least, it will place each child's reading level in a comparative relationship with national and world standards. Often, individualized reading programs allow for no comparisons of a child's progress, comprehension skills, or versatility in dealing with subject matters through reading and writing. Too often, the teacher in individualized programs becomes a prisoner of the child's momentary interests. It is, after all, a child-centered program, isn't it?

However, the positive side of a good individualized program is that it can allow for the time and leisure to read good literature away from classroom texts, as integral masterpieces that the child experiences as a totality. There also should be time and flexibility in a well-planned individualized program to utilize a wide variety of computer programs. These programs, along with various multimedia experiences—CD-Roms, for example—aid reading and writing skills for comprehension and they enrich all subject matters, including the basal reading program.

The danger in any whole language program in the language arts is that under the stress of complexity, with the teacher dealing with too many individual curricula in one classroom, some children will get short shrift. Such children's personal difficulties must be addressed and remediated, and programs must move ahead rapidly enough to fit their individual learning potentialities.

The difficulty with individualized reading programs, as part of the whole language philosophy, is that they presume that all the twenty-five or so children in a classroom will be on a generally equal ability level. Usually, especially in the average public school classroom, the differences between the children are too wide for the teacher to function well for all the children without using some grouping or other structural mechanism for the reading and language arts program.

If the basal is used as the fulcrum of the reading program—consider the basals' extremely attractive formats, written, as they are, by experts from real schools, by professors as well as creative writers—the child could be well-served.

There is good reason for the elementary and secondary curriculum to articulate and require a clearly enunciated program of study. This mean more than subject matter ordered by level of difficulty. Even more important for the elementary child is that there be a conscious skill- and comprehension-based sequence in language learning. Finally, all observed deviations from expected rates and levels of learning in the child ought to be immediately recognized and communicated by the educational authorities.

Momentarily, the process of interdiction and remediation ought to begin to ensure that the child can be gotten back onto the path of success. Parent knowledge of all phases of the reading program, and their child's progress within it, is a justified demand by the "home front."

# Chapter 13

# *What Parents Can Do*

## POSSIBILITIES

An intellectually literate family environment is the ideal. When this sort of environment is a natural outgrowth of the lives of adult family members it is all the more likely that the youngsters will follow. Parents and educators should remember that such environments are not merely artificial creations produced with the stimulus of some razzle-dazzle television personality urging parents on to high moral behavior.

We are biological creatures with inborn tendencies and aptitudes. Thus, even as we biologically create a child to live within our family, we also biologically endow the child with our inclinations to "go for" those same interests that induced our own parents to create that environment of books, conversation, intellectual outlooks that we want our children to absorb and profit from.

The world is "going intellectual" in an outburst of modernization. Those without the reading and writing skills that are necessary for the computers and other high-tech dimensions of this ever more

abstract world community will be left behind. They will be remain-
dered to devour the crumbs flung out by those who can think, read,
write, and thus shape this world-in-the-making.

Can every child and family aspire to full participation in this new
world? No one can answer that question about even any one
particular set of parents or children. The similarity from father and
mother to children exists, but often the phenomenon of regression
to the mean occurs: Parents with high ability meet, marry, and
reproduce. Husband and wife, unaffiliated humans, have IQs and
educations that are often more similar than brothers and sisters.
Yet the probability that two highly skilled parents will have equally
highly skilled children is not absolute. (Remember, Aunt Jennie and
Cousin Rudy are also in the family!) Thus, children often fail to
satisfy the expectations of their parents and teachers.

However, as they dote on the gurgles of their little Norman or
Nancy, Mother and Father should begin to search for ways to develop
that unknown possibility and potential inherent in their children.
Parents have the power to determine the extent that this inborn
potential can go to work for these unique humans-in-the-making.

No school or teacher, reading curriculum or program, even pile
of tutoring or enrichment monies, is as important as what goes on
spontaneously as life within the family. For the child, this set of
intimate realities is the greatest educator.

## EDUCATIONAL PARTNERS

There is no question that parents and schools should be at least
coequals in the important decision making that affects a child's
literacy future. Unfortunately, many families have no choices as to
their children's teachers, or as to what philosophy the schools use
in picking out the books that the children will read or the ideas and
values that the children will absorb in their most dominating
external social environment outside the family—the school and its
classrooms.

This is why upward of one million parents assume the responsibility for literacy and educational progress by tutoring their
children at home, undergoing the double burden of public school
taxes and loss of family income that often result. Whether children
learn their academics at home or in a public, private, or parochial
school, parents should never think of their job as finished.

**Table 13.1**
**Parents, Children, and Literacy: Pointers**

---

**Children Reading to Parents**

*Something for You to Do at Home!*

Beginning today, your child is bringing home a reader with a particular page assigned for the purpose of *practicing oral reading*. You may have him/her read any other story or all of the stories if you wish, but on Friday the assigned page must be read for an oral reading grade.

The book which is being brought home is one level below your child's reading group level; therefore, it should be easy to read. Listed below are the areas that will be considered:

1. Reads with proper expression (shows excitement, questioning, etc.).
2. Pauses for commas and dashes.
3. Stops at periods and question marks.
4. Reads in phrases and not by individual words.
5. Does not omit or change words.
6. Does not go back and repeat a word or begin again at the start of a sentence.
7. Pronounces the endings of words such as book*s* and go*ing*.

*Enjoy reading with your child!*

---

Of course, reading to children and surrounding them with books, newspapers, and magazines are important. More important are the intangibles of family conversations and adult interests as shared with children. It is often a shock to parents to realize how much a child can pick up in the garage while Father works on the car, or from Mother as she discusses financial decisions with the broker.

Politics, the arts, and sports are interests that can lead children to a leaf through a newspaper on their own. The key is to make available publications that are somewhat challenging to the reading skills of the child. For up to third grade, the local newspaper and its fourth-grade vocabulary will probably suffice. For something a bit more interesting and educationally useful, national or specialized newspapers and magazines may be necessary.

**Table 13.2**
**What Parents Can Do to Promote Literacy**

1.  Promote a love of reading by surrounding the child with things to read such as books, newspapers, and magazines.

2.  Use teachers as resources for appropriate reading materials and ideas for writing activities.

3.  Limit TV viewing. Although it may bring the child into contact with popular culture, it does not develop thinking skills.

4.  Make reading a family activity through bedtimes stories and other special reading times. Let the child take turns reading.

In the case of more school-oriented concerns, the parent could consult the reading coordinator in the local school district for more challenging texts in reading and writing, asking what literature the teachers are using to reach their own understanding of the children's progress in reading. Especially important would be texts that describe the various subject matter skills and conceptual tools that are necessary for reading for meaning, for which many children need extra help.

A wide variety of such texts is available. Parents need not have the child actually go through the exercises—underlining the main idea of a paragraph, or consulting the dictionary for the meaning of two or three words in a subject matter chapter. Rather, they could use these texts to stimulate their own ideas for new ways to work with their children. Such work, carried out in a game-like environment, could encourage the children to learn more, to accomplish ever more challenging tasks.

The history of important achievements by youngsters—they need not all be prodigies—through strong parental input, argues for an activist family role in the education of every child. Simply, parents need to ask themselves how important is parent-stimulated achievement? Given equal potential (test scores) in children, there are still many factors, especially in talent and personality, that can modify their performance success. Only the parent can evaluate these subtleties. Teachers are much too overworked to touch more than the bare surfaces of individual differences, let alone probe the deeper psychological, or even the learning styles and modalities through which children learn.

This is why we have stressed the importance of the reading system in the child's transition to fluent reading from decoding written material to their rough sound equivalents. Each child is different and will make the transition at various stages of development. Other highly intelligent children will never be natural readers. They will have to find other ways to access their deeper potentialities. Often these children, some dyslexic, others borderline readers, will find more powerful successes in mathematics, art, music, business, and many other educationally important dimensions of learning.

The goal for every parent is to mine and educate his child's inner intellectual potential. The performance vehicles of this release are not crucial as long as there remains a social use or market for these skills. The world needs highly able humans for a wide variety of tasks. The secure minimum competency jobs do not exist anymore. There are many MBAs on the floor of auto plants today. The search is always for the best educated and most competent. Therefore, parents need to encourage their children to develop their most powerful vehicle for exercising deep-structured intelligence. Parents also should never be bashful in seeking outside counsel and concrete assistance.

Every child needs help in this long-enduring task. Even for ordinary potential, to find an educational pathway for developing one's "best thing" could mean the difference between a life of fulfillment and one of embitterment and social isolation.

## TELEVISION

For the education of your child, television is probably the second-most important dilemma, the first being friends and activities outside the home, which will be discussed below.

No question, television is an opportunity for both enrichment and disaster. For most of the young adult generation, television has opened up a vast world of information and factual knowledge about the lives of humans, animals, and the physical environment. Our access to cultural personalities, drama, and even some good entertainment, cannot be questioned.

Yet the controversy continues about the impact of television on youngsters, let alone on the cultural ambience of our society. It continues despite the fact that, according to government reports, the more television children watch, the poorer their reading abilities are likely to be, as tested by national and international yardsticks of achievement.

Yes, of course, in well-guided and minimal clumps of exposure, television for children can be an enriching supplement. The visual images of a world outside can break down the boundaries of social and economic ghettos. The poor all over the world opt for a television and antenna before they demand indoor plumbing. It is a humanizing contact with a world beyond. It is also a stimulus to join the larger society. For middle-class American children, the situation is somewhat different. In theory they should have had a fair amount of contact with the outside world.

The United States has been wealthy for a much longer time than the vast majority of the nations of the world. Our present challenge is to keep up with the modernizing nations of the world, and not to descend to Third-World status. This thought is important today because of the abysmally low rates of highly competent readers—somewhere between 4 and 9 percent of our high-school seniors, depending on how the statistics are interpreted.

Youngsters who land in this higher group of literacy-competent people will be able to join the internationally skilled social classes of the future. They will not only be able to select the finest colleges of their choice, they will likely be able to move into positions of responsibility in those governmental, corporate, educational, and cultural/scientific professions that require the best.

A diet of television will not help a child become a highly competent reader, with all the promise that holds. The fundamental reasons for this are probably neurological and medical, still unclear in their full operation and meaning. Yet I believe it can be summarized succinctly and briefly, as follows.

Information gathering through television watching is a basically visual operation, operating off the same structure of information processing as sitting on one's porch and casually observing the events along the block. As has been stated before, television elicits a passive response, often acting as a behavioral sedative—or a cheap babysitter for the kids.

Reading a book or newspaper, by contrast, is active. The mind has to translate the symbolic scrawls of print into a structure of

**Table 13.3**
**Television Sources for Parents**

ABC Community Relations; ABC-TV; 1330 Avenue of the Americas; New York,
NY 10019–5402

CBS Television Reading Program; 51 West 52 Street; New York, NY 10019–6010

NBC Parent Participation Workshops; Teachers Guide to Television; 699 Madison
Avenue; New York, NY 10021

Action for Children's Television; 46 Austin Street; Newtonville, MA 02160

Parent-Teacher's Association; 700 N. Rush Street; Chicago, IL 60611

Prime-Time; 120 LaSalle Street; Chicago IL 60603

National Council for Children and Television; 20 Nassau Street; Princeton, NJ
08540

meaning. To read is to think. It may be rapid skimming or slow step-by-step thinking through difficult technical material. The fully functioning reading system makes rapid skimming possible. But in both cases, in fast as well as slow reading, the mind, deep-structured intellect, has to be mobilized.

In watching television, this is not necessarily the case. Our brain is structured in such a way that even though the letters and word symbols that we read are passed through our visual systems, they are rapidly transferred away from the purely object-oriented image system of ordinary visual and television experience. What emerges from reading is a new nonvisual pattern of thought that can act as the gatekeeper for a wide variety of thinking processes.

Think of the rapid reading of Braille by the blind. Here the shapes of letters and words that the blind touch bypass the visual system. They are passed immediately from touch by the fingers through a different neurological system into the mind, and toward meaning.

Reading competency becomes important, therefore, because it can help a youngster into the role of slow and careful analysis and relational thinking that are at the heart of mathematics, computers, musical notation, and a host of other and derivative abstract skills. Without such skills, youngsters are prepared for little more than part-time work at a fast food restaurant, or some other minimum-wage job.

The crux of the "TV and children problem" lies in family and parental standards, and how they will be exercised for long-term benefit of the child. Some minimum level of television, especially if it is monitored to include educational and other valuable viewing, is positive. Nowadays, much classroom activity revolves around the expectation that all families have televisions—although some families, of course, ban televisions from their homes—and that children watch television a fairly large percentage of the time. The parent can be held prisoner by such expectations. But parents can tell the school authorities what they think of such matters.

When the benefits and deficits of television are toted up, I would argue that less is more. The reading of novels and history, nature, and science materials requires large expenditures of time. A home where the family spends time reading as opposed to masquerading as couch potatoes is a place of education and "becoming." Children of such families have greater opportunities to become thinkers and doers. They will more likely look forward to taking control of their lives through the knowledge instrumentalities available to them.

Therefore, count mine as one vote *contra* TV, except for the special occasion.


## OUTSIDE: THE ULTIMATE CHALLENGE

Without question, most parents have lost control of their children's destiny by the time the children enter high school. The temptations of early maturity, the glitter and excitement of ordinary existence in modern-day affluence, have wrenched many children from the ambience of home into a world of friends and frenzy.

For the child, it is great fun to participate in the daily games and interactions of life in the peer group. There the world is seemingly *at hand*, offering information and experiences far more inviting outside the home than within. But also, it is a world in which the family is no longer a primary institution for protecting and rearing the child. The state and the school, the vast armada of social service agencies, can early provide the atmosphere for an immature youngster's rebelliousness.

The family in the United States seems to be in a state of disintegration at this crucial time when the nation more than ever needs the family to survive. It is ironic to see a society self-destruct at the very time that it is politically undermining the foundations of the institution—the nuclear family—that might save it. How could the nuclear family save our country? By being once again the basis for the education and flourishing of the incoming generation of leaders and builders.

The message to any family that wishes the best for its children, both today and tomorrow, is simple: Fight! Don't let the streets take over your destiny. Oversee your children's morality and educational ideals. Be aware of your children's friends. It's up to you, not the outside world, to guide your family. If you do struggle to maintain the ideals of your family for your children, you may be surprised to discover that many others feel the same as you do. Their and your children will come together to form the backbone of a new cohort of the competent.

Your vigilance in watching over your children's reading program can become part of this overall process of supervision and nurturing, which should extend throughout *all* the years, even into maturity.

If you want your child to become a reader, and then a thinker, you will have to be both tenacious and resourceful in providing the time and opportunity for such activity. As parents, we all hope that the process will grow internally. As children discover the power inherent in reading, they may find on their own that reading interesting and emotionally and intellectually powerful material is preferable to the transitory boredom of the tube, or even a Saturday-night party. The latter is, of course, not bad, on occasion. But too often for the youngsters, the party becomes the norm and continues, through inertia, into perpetual entertainment.

There is a dilemma here. There are many successful parents who, for one reason or another—perhaps when they were young, their noses were held too closely to the grindstone—feel that they must relieve their own children from the regimen of a taskmaster. Accordingly, they do little to motivate or discipline their children. Children are often lost this way, both for the present and the future. On the other hand, there are parents who exploit a child's gifts, often for naught, because the youngster has been the unwilling pawn in the parents' power play for their own economic benefit (sports parents). The child's inner will dries up, and the great and prodigal achievements disappear in a blink.

The balance between providing stimulation and motivation and being overly rigid is fluid. How much should the parents push, and how hard, for the achievements to flow? How long can the stimulus and the discipline continue before the internal motivation issues spontaneously from the child herself? These are important questions. A child will become an adult. Denial of the stretched-out periods of play and fun before the reckoning of adult life could raise the inevitable question: Why were such valuable years frittered away?

## THE TALENTS OF CHILDREN

At twelve or thirteen years of age, children begin to come into their biological maturity. They also begin to give parents an idea of their educational potential. This potential should be seen as: (1) basic academic ability and general intelligence, and (2) special talents and interests. Nothing is yet fixed in stone. Some youngsters don't show their talents until well into adolescence. Parents are honor-bound to be realists, but ever hopeful and enterprising in doing the rational best for their young. This means, don't give up!

In considering reading and language skills, the parent should understand that these are important surface talents, behind which lies children's bubbling intelligence. Children may be good in some or all aspects of the four language modalities, speaking, listening, reading, and writing, or they may not be good in any. Remember that some of the most fluent speakers, people with phenomenal abilities to remember names and events, can be only empty shells. They have all the various verbal skills, but these don't help if one has nothing to say.

Other youngsters, who are practically mute, who may be interested in neither reading nor writing, can show enormous talents in math, music, or art. Sometimes these youngsters—Albert Einstein is an example—show little interest in the literary world of words and carve out enormously successful careers in science and engineering. Others, when they discover an overriding passion, can skillfully transfer mediocre existing reading and writing skills to

great success in fields such as business or medicine. Not everyone
has to be a lawyer or an English professor.

Let us reiterate, good readers often will not be good natural
writers. They will struggle—endlessly write and rewrite—in order
to develop their skills. This applies to all aspects of literacy, as well
as to other fields, for example, the physics theoretician is not always
the good experimenter.

Parents should seriously and objectively evaluate their children
at ages twelve to thirteen. This is the age when the hunt for gifted
children begins. Before this age, children are extremely malleable.
They are too immature for anyone to make any long-term predictions for them. Therefore, be wary of any IQ test scores of children
before age twelve. Such scores do *not* predict future potentiality
with any surety as compared with tests administered at the beginning and throughout the adolescent years.

Why is this life moment so important? Adolescence is a word
that should give away the answer. Children change at this stage in
their intellectual and emotional valences. Their personalities begin
to take shape, and their basic persistence drives either continue or
wither. Many an astounding prodigy has faded with adolescence.
The development of the sexual persona into a mature and self-de-
termining human can alter both the intellectual and/or talent
exceptionality, which often, of course, was created by a parent.

The converse is also true. Youngsters of no special abilities often
take hold, refute all of their teachers' and parents' smug denigra-
tions, and storm into the future, exhibiting skills as wondrous as
they are surprising.

At this point in the education of the child, the secondary school
years, the parent is inevitably going to lose the kind of control that
they had when the youngster was in elementary school. Now the
choice of school becomes crucial. Many parents have discovered
that of all the schools their children have attended, from nursery
school up to graduate school, the most important is the secondary
school, the high school.

Psychologists often cite the period from fourteen to sixteen years
of age as the time when the brain reaches its highest level of early
maturity. This is why we often find chess international grand
masters as young as fifteen years of age. Chess is a game of mind,
speed, and energy. Adolescents have this boiling mental as well as
sexual energy running through them. A fine high school—public,
independent, or parochial—will be able to tap into this mental

energy and direct the child into intellectual involvements in subject matter areas that excite them.

Because human ability and talent rest on a core of general intelligence that is usually thought of as being measured by IQ tests, they can be channeled into many subject matter byways, often depending on the unique talents of the young person. A stimulating and gifted teacher can guide the student into areas of potentiality, sometimes into wholly new disciplines, fields that are just beginning to open up.

The key is to find the high school that will build on the skills for learning that the child has acquired in grade school, and shape these skills into a whole new repertoire of guided and independent learning styles. It is the study skills that are internalized during the period from fourteen to eighteen years of age that will probably be the most powerful gift for the individual as she grows into full maturity.

# For Further Reading

## CHAPTER 1

### Baby Speaks

Berk, L. E. 1993. *Infants, Children, and Adolescents.* Boston: Allyn and Bacon.

Crain-Thoreson, C., and Dale, P. S. 1992. "Do Early Talkers Become Early Readers?" *Developmental Psychology* 28: 421–429.

de Villiers, J. G., and de Villiers, P. A. 1978. *Language Acquisition.* Cambridge, MA: Harvard University Press.

Greene, M.C.L. 1960. *Learning to Talk.* New York: Harper & Brothers.

Jones, M. V. 1972. *Language Development: The Key to Learning.* Springfield, IL: Charles C. Thomas Publishers.

Kavanagh, J. F., and Mattingly, I. G., eds. 1972. *Language by Ear and by Eye: The Relationships Between Speech and Reading.* Cambridge, MA: MIT Press.

Lamb, P., ed. 1967. *Guiding Children's Language Learning.* Dubuque, IO: William C. Brown.

Leach, P. 1983. *Babyhood.* New York: Alfred A. Knopf.

Locke, J. L. 1993. *The Child's Path to Spoken Language.* Cambridge, MA: Harvard University Press.

Moerk, E. L. 1992. *First Language: Taught and Learned.* Baltimore, MD: Paul H. Brookes.

Petty, W. T., and Jensen, J. M. 1980. *Developing Children's Language.* Boston: Allyn and Bacon.

Rentel, V. M., Corson, S. A., and Dunn, B., eds. 1985. *Psychophysiological Aspects of Reading and Learning.* New York: Gordon and Breach Scientific Publishers.

Schickedanz, J. A. 1990. *Adams Righting Revolutions: One Child's Literacy Development from Infancy through Grade One.* Portsmouth, NH: Heinemann.

Trantham, C. R., and Pedersen, J. K. 1976. *Normal Language Development: The Key to Diagnosis and Therapy for Language-Disordered Children.* Baltimore, MD: Williams and Wilkins Company.

## CHAPTER 2

### Our Alphabet: Language by Ear and by Eye

Adams, M. J. 1990. *Beginning to Read: Thinking and Learning About Print.* Cambridge, MA: MIT Press.

Ball, E. W. 1993. "Assessing Phonemic Awareness." *Language, Speech, and Hearing Services in School* 24.

Bentin, S. 1992. "Phonological Awareness, Reading, and Reading Acquisition: A Survey and Appraisal of Current Knowledge." *Haskins Laboratories Status Report on Speech Research* SR 111/112: 167–180.

Boloz, S. A. 1994. "Supporting Emergent Literacy Is Everyone's Responsibility." *Reading Teacher* 47: 388–390.

Bradley, L., and Bryant, P. E. 1983. "Categorizing Sounds and Learning to Read—A Causal Connection." *Nature* 301: 419–421.

Brady, S. A., and Shankweiler, D. P., eds. 1991. *Phonological Processes in Literacy.* Hillsdale, NJ: Lawrence Erlbaum Assoc.

Byrne, B., and Barnsley, R. 1989. "Phonemic Awareness and Letter Knowledge in the Child's Acquisition of Phoneme Identity." *Journal of Educational Psychology* 81: 313–321.

Byrne, B., and Barnsley, R. 1990. "Acquiring the Alphabet Principle: A Case for Teaching Recognition of Phoneme Identity." *Journal of Educational Psychology* 82: 850–812.

Byrne, B., and Barnsley, R. 1991. "Evaluation of a Program to Teach Phonemic Awareness to Young Children." *Journal of Educational Psychology* 83: 451–455.

Gough, P. B., and Hillenger, M. L. 1980. "Learning to Read: An Unnatural Act." *Bulletin of the Orton Society* 30: 180–196.

Griffith, P. L., and Klesius, J. P. 1992. "Kindergarten Children's Developing Understanding of the Alphabetic Principle." Paper presented at the annual meeting of the National Reading Conference, San Antonio, TX.

Kavanagh, J. F., and Mattingly, I. G., eds. 1972. *Language by Ear and by Eye*. Cambridge, MA: MIT Press.

Klesius, J. P. 1991. "A Whole Language and Traditional Comparison: Overall Effectiveness and Development of the Alphabetic Principle." *Reading Research and Instruction* 30: 47–61.

Mann, V. A. 1993. "Phoneme Awareness and Future Reading Ability." *Journal of Learning Disabilities* 26(4): 259–269.

Pond, M. 1993. "Emergent Literacy in Early Childhood Programs." *Ohio Reading Teacher* 27: 7–10.

Reutzal, D. R. 1992. "Breaking the Letter-a-Week Tradition: Conveying the Alphabetic Principle to Young Children." *Childhood Education* 69: 20–23.

Teale, W. H. 1984. "Reading to Young Children: Its Significance for Literacy Development." In *Awakening to Literacy*, H. Goelman, A. Oberg, and F. Smith, eds. Portsmouth, NH: Heinemann.

Teale, W. H., and Chittenden, E. 1987. "Assessing Young Children's Literacy Development." *Reading Teacher* 40: 772–776.

## CHAPTER 3

### Preparing Your Child to Read

Adams, M. J. 1991. "Beginning to Read: A Critique by Literacy Professionals and a Response by Marilyn Jager Adams." *Reading Teacher* 44: 6.

Bagford, J. 1968. "Reading Readiness Scores and Success in Reading." *Reading Teacher* 21: 324–328.

Ball, E. W., and Blachman, B. A. 1988. "Phoneme Segmentation Training: Effect on Reading Readiness." *Annals of Dyslexia* 38: 208–225.

Bradley, L., and Bryant, P. E. 1983. "Categorizing Sounds and Learning to Read—A Causal Connection." *Nature* 301: 419–421.

Catts, H. 1991. "Facilitating Phonemic Awareness." *Language, Speech, and Hearing Services in Schools* 22.

Clark, M. 1976. *Young Fluent Readers*. London: Heinemann.

Clay, M. 1982. *Observing Young Readers*. Portsmouth, NH: Heinemann.

Cunningham, A. E. 1990. "Explicit Versus Implicit Instruction in Phonemic Awareness." *Journal of Experimental Child Psychology* 50: 429–444.

Durkin, D. 1966. *Children Who Read Early*. New York: Teachers College Press.

Durkin, D. 1989. *New Kindergarten Basal Reader Materials: What's a Teacher Supposed to Do with All This?* (Tech. Rep. #475). Urbana-Champaign, IL: University of Illinois, Center for the Study of Reading.

Fields, M. V., Spangler, K. L., and Lee, D. M. 1991. *Let's Begin Reading Right: Developmentally Appropriate Beginning Literacy*, 2nd ed. New York: Macmillan.

Foorman, B. R., and Siegel, A. W., eds. 1986. *Acquisition of Reading Skills*. Hillsdale, NJ: Lawrence Erlbaum Assoc.

Genishi, C., and Dyson, A. H., 1984. *Language Assessment in the Early Years*. Norwood, NJ: Ablex.

Gibson, E. J. 1965. "Learning to Read." *Science* 148: 1066–1072.

Gillingham, A., and Stillman, B. W. 1966. *Remedial Training for Children with Specific Difficulties in Reading, Spelling and Phonetics*. Cambridge, MA: Education Publishing Service.

Gredler, G. 1978. "A Look at Some Important Factors for Assessing Reading Readiness for School." *Journal of Learning Disabilities* 11: 284–290.

Henig, R. M. 1988. "Should Baby Read?" *New York Times Magazine*, 22 May: 37–38.

Hildreth, G. 1950. *Readiness for School Beginners*. New York: Harcourt Brace.

Jackson, N. E. 1988. "Precocious Reading Ability: What Does it Mean?" *Gifted-Child Quarterly* 32: 200–204.

Jackson, N. E., Donaldson, G. W., and Cleland, L. N. 1988. "The Structure of Precocious Reading Ability." *Journal of Educational Psychology* 30: 234–243.

Kasten, W. C., and Clarke, B. K. 1989. *Reading/Writing Readiness for Preschool and Kindergarten Children: A Whole Language Approach.* Florida Educational Research Council Research Project Report. Sarasota, FL: University of South Florida.

Katz, L. G. 1990. "Should Preschoolers Learn the Three R's?" *Parents' Magazine* 65: 206.

Kutner, L. 1994. "Getting Ready for Reading." *Parent's Magazine* 69: 72–74.

Lundberg, I., Frost, J., Petersen, O.-P. 1988. "Effects of an Extensive Program for Stimulating Phonological Awareness in Preschool Children." *Reading Research Quarterly* 23(3): 263–283.

Maclean, M., Bryant, P., and Bradley, L. 1987. "Rhymes, Nursery Rhymes, and Reading in Early Childhood." *Merrill-Palmer Quarterly* 33: 255–281.

Mason, J. M. 1980. "When Do Children Begin to Read: An Exploration of Four-year-old Children's Letter and Word Reading Competencies." *Reading Research Quarterly* 15: 203–227.

*Metropolitan Early School Inventory—Preliteracy.* 1986. Orlando, FL: The Psychological Corporation of Harcourt Brace Jovanovich.

Nurss, J. R. 1979. "Assessment of Readiness." In *Reading Research: Advances in Theory and Practice,* G. E. MacKinnon and T. G. Waller, eds. New York: Academic Press.

Orton, S. 1966. "The Orton-Gillingham Approach." In *the Disabled Reader,* J. Money, ed. Baltimore, MD: Johns Hopkins University Press.

Pflaum, S. W. 1978. *The Development of Language and Reading in Young Children.* Columbus, OH: Merrill.

Roberts, F. 1988. "Are Early Readers Bored in School?" *Parents' Magazine* 63: 48.

Schwartz, J. I. 1988. *Encouraging Early Literacy: An Integrated Approach to Reading and Writing in N-3.* Portsmouth, NH: Heinemann.

Tangel, D. M., and Blanchman, B. A. 1992. "Effect of Phoneme Awareness Instruction on Kindergarten Children's Invented Spelling." *Journal of Reading Behavior* 24: 233–261.

Teale, W. H. 1984. "Reading to Young Children: Its Significance for Literacy Development." In *Awakening to Literacy*, H. Goelman, A. Oberg, and F. Smith, eds. Portsmouth, NH: Heinemann.

Wedell, K. 1970. "Perceptuo-Motor Factors." *Journal of Special Education* 4: 3.


## CHAPTER 4

## Slow Reading: Phonics and Decoding

Adams, M. J. 1991. "Why Not Phonics and Whole Language?" *All Language and the Creation of Literacy*. Baltimore, MD: Orton Dyslexia Society.

Anderson, W. W., and Fordham, A. E. 1991. "Issues in Education: Beware of 'Magic' Phonics Programs." *Childhood Education* 68: 8–9.

Aukerman, R. C. 1984. *Approaches to Beginning Reading*, 2nd ed. New York: John Wiley and Sons.

Blumenfeld, S. 1973. *The New Illiterates*. New York: Arlington House.

Brady, S. A. 1986. "Short Term Memory, Phonological Processing, and Reading Ability." *Annals of Dyslexia* 36: 138–153.

Chall, J. 1983. *Learning to Read: The Great Debate*, rev. ed. New York: McGraw-Hill.

Copperman, P. 1980. *The Literacy Hoax*. New York: Morrow-Quill.

Dolch, E., and Bloomster, M. 1937. "Phonic Readiness." *Elementary School Journal* 38: 201–205.

Dreyer, L. G. 1989. "The Relationship of Children's Phonological Memory to Decoding and Reading Ability." Doctoral Dissertation, Columbia University, *Dissertation Abstracts International* 89: B2451.

Ehri, L. C., and Robbins, C. 1992. "Beginners Need Some Decoding Skills to Read Words by Analogy." *Reading Research Quarterly* 27: 13–26.

Fields, M. V. 1987. *Let's Begin Reading Right: A Developmental Approach to Beginning Literacy*. Columbus, OH: Merrill.

Flesch, R. 1955. *Why Johnny Can't Read and What You Can Do About it*. New York: Harper.

Goswami, U., and Bryant, P. 1990. *Phonological Skills and Learning to Read*. Hillsdale, NJ: Lawrence Erlbaum Assoc.

Torgesen, J. K., Morgan, S. T., and Davis, C. 1992. "Effects of Two Types of Phonological Awareness Training on Word Learning in Kindergarten Children." *Journal of Educational Psychology* 84(3): 364–370.

Vellutino, F. R., and Scanlon, D. M. 1987. "Phonological Coding, Phonological Awareness, and Reading Ability: Evidence from a Longitudinal Study." *Merrill-Palmer Quarterly* 33(3): 321–363.

## CHAPTER 5

### The Child's Reading System

Adams, M. J. 1990. *Beginning to Read: Thinking and Learning About Print*. Urbana-Champaign, IL: Reading Research and Education Center, Center for the Study of Reading, University of Illinois.

Anderson, J. 1977. "Neural Models with Cognitive Implications." In *Basic Processes of Reading*, D. LaBarge and S. Samuels, eds. Hillsdale, NJ: Lawrence Erlbaum Assoc.

Chall, J. 1983. *Stages of Reading Development*. New York: McGraw Hill.

Downing, J. A. 1979. *Reading and Reasoning*. New York: Springer-Verlag.

Ellis, A. W. 1984. *Reading, Writing and Dyslexia: A Cognitive Analysis*. London: Lawrence Erlbaum Assoc.

Fries, C., Fries, A. C., Wilson, R. G., and Rudolph, M. K., eds. 1966. *Merrill Linguistic Readers*. Columbus, OH: Charles E. Merrill Books.

Gates, A. 1937. "The Necessary Mental Age for Beginning Reading." *Elementary School Journal* 37: 497–508.

Geschwind, N. 1982. "Why Orton Was Right." *Annals of Dyslexia* 32: 13–30.

Gibson, E. J. 1965. "Learning to Read." *Science* 148: 1066–1072.

Gibson, E. J. 1970. "The Ontogeny of Reading." *American Psychologist* 25: 136–142.

Gibson, E. J., and Levin, H. 1975. *The Psychology of Reading*. Cambridge, MA: MIT Press.

Golden, R. M. 1986. "A Developmental, Neural Model of Visual Word Perception." *Cognitive Science* 10(3): 241–276.

Huey, E. B. 1968. *The Psychology and Pedagogy of Reading* [1908]. Cambridge, MA: MIT Press.

Itzkoff, S. W. 1986. *How We Learn to Read*. Ashfield, MA: Paideia Publishers.

Juel, C., Griffith, P. L., and Gough, P. B. 1986. "Acquisition of Literacy: A Longitudinal Study of Children in First and Second Grade." *Journal of Educational Psychology* 78: 243–255.

Just, M. A., and Carpenter, P. A. 1987. *The Psychology of Reading and Language Comprehension*. Boston: Allyn and Bacon.

Mason, J. M. 1976. "Overgeneralization in Learning to Read." *Journal of Reading Behavior* 8: 173–182.

Mazurkiewicz, A. J., ed. 1966. *I.T.A. and the World of English*. Hempstead, NY: ITA Foundation.

McCracken, G., and Walcutt, C. C. 1963. *Lippincott's Basic Reading*. Philadelphia: J. B. Lippincott.

Morphett, M. V., and Washburne, C. 1931. "When Should Children Begin to Read?" *Elementary School Journal* 31: 495–503.

Oakhill, J., and Gamham, A. 1988. *Becoming a Skilled Reader*. New York: HarperCollins.

Orton, S. 1937. *Reading, Writing, and Speech Problems in Children*. New York: W. W. Norton.

Samuels, S. J. 1985. "Automaticity and Repeated Reading." In *Reading Education: Foundations for a Literate America*, J. Osborn, P. T. Wilson, and R. C. Anderson, eds. Lexington, MA: Lexington Books.

Smith, F. 1994. *Understanding Reading*, 4th ed. Hillsdale, NJ: Lawrence Erlbaum Assoc.

Smith, F., ed. 1973. *Psycholinguistics and Reading*. New York: Holt, Rinehart and Winston. (See "Decoding: The Great Fallacy," pp. 70–83.)

Torrey, J. W. 1969. "Learning to Read Without a Teacher: A Case Study." *Elementary English* 46: 550–556.

Yuill, N. 1991. *Children's Problems in Text Comprehension: An Experimental Investigation.* New York: Cambridge University Press.

## CHAPTER 6

### Reading Is Understanding

Adams, J. 1986. *The Conspiracy of the Text.* New York: Routledge and Kegan Paul.

Atwood, B. S. 1975. *Developing Skills in Critical Reading.* Palo Alto, CA: Learning Handbooks.

Bettleheim, B., and Zelan, K. 1982. *On Learning to Read: The Child's Fascination with Meaning.* New York: Knopf.

Brown, A. L., Campione, J. C., and Day, J. D. 1981. "Learning to Learn: On Training Students to Learn from Texts." *Educational Researcher* 10: 14–21.

Carver, R. P. 1981. *Reading Comprehension and Theory.* Springfield, IL: Thomas.

Clay, M. 1976. *Reading: The Patterning of Complex Behaviour.* Auckland, NZ: Heinemann.

Downing, J. 1979. *Reading and Reasoning.* New York: Springer-Verlag.

Durkin, D. 1978–1979. "What Classroom Observations Reveal About Reading Comprehension Instruction." *Reading Research Quarterly* 14: 481–533.

Feathers, K. M. 1993. *Infotext: Reading and Learning.* Markham, Ont.: Pippen Publishers.

Gates, A. I. 1928. *New Methods in Primary Reading.* New York: Columbia University Press.

Gibson, E. J. 1970. "The Ontogeny of Reading." *American Psychologist* 25: 136–142.

Goodman, Y. M., and Burke, C., with Sherman, B. 1980. *Reading Strategies: Focus on Comprehension.* New York: Holt, Rinehart, and Winston.

Irwin, J. W. 1991. *Teaching Reading Comprehension Processes.* Englewood Cliffs, NJ: Prentice Hall.

Irwin, J. W., and Baker, I. 1989. *Promoting Active Reading Comprehension Strategies.* Englewood Cliffs, NJ: Prentice Hall.

Iwicki, A. L. 1992. "Vocabulary Connections." *Reading Teacher* 45: 736.

Johnston, P. 1983. *Reading Comprehension Assessment: A Cognitive Basis.* Newark, DE: International Reading Association.

Just, M. A., and Carpenter, P. A. 1987. *The Psychology of Reading and Language Comprehension.* Boston: Allyn and Bacon.

Olson, M. W., and Gee, T. 1991. "Content Reading Instruction in the Primary Grades: Perceptions and Strategies." *Reading Teacher* 45: 298–307.

Pearson, P. D. 1984. "The Comprehension Revolution: A Twenty-Year History of Process and Practice Related to Reading Comprehension." In *Contexts of School-Based Literacy,* T. E. Raphael and R. E. Reynolds, eds. New York: Longman.

Pearson, P. D., and Fielding, L. G. 1991. "Comprehension Instruction." In *Handbook of Reading Research,* R. Barr, M. L. Kamil, P. B. Mosenthal, and P. D. Pearson, eds. New York: Longman.

Pearson, P. D., and Johnson, D. 1978. *Teaching Reading Comprehension.* New York: Holt, Rinehart, and Winston.

Schell, L. 1988. "Dilemmas in Assessing Reading Comprehension." *Reading Teacher* 42: 12–16.

Sternberg, R. J., 1991. "Are We Reading Too Much into Reading Comprehension Tests?" *Journal of Reading* 34: 540–454.

Tierney, R. J., Readence, J. E., and Dishner, E. K., 1990. *Reading Strategies and Practices: A Compendium.* Boston: Allyn and Bacon.

Torrey, J. W. 1969. "Learning to Read Without a Teacher: A Case Study." *Elementary English* 46: 550–556.

Vacca, R. T., and Vacca, J. L. 1989. *Content Area Reading.* Glenview, IL: Scott, Foresman.

Wepman, J. M. 1964. "The Perceptual Basis for Learning." *Reading and the Language Arts.* Chicago: University of Chicago Press, 25–33.

## CHAPTER 7

### First Grade Rubicon: Ten Important Tips

Bridge, C. A., Winograd, P. N., and Healey, D. 1983. "Using Predictable Materials to Teach Beginning Reading." *Reading Teacher* 36: 884–891.

Carnine, D., Kameenui, E., and Coyle, G. 1984. "Utilization of Contextual Information in Determining the Meaning of Unfamiliar Words (Study 2)." *Reading Research Quarterly* 19: 188–204.

Carnine, E., Silbert, J., and Kameenui, E. 1990. *Direct Instruction in Reading*. Columbus, OH: Merrill.

Clarke, L. K. 1988. "Invented Versus Traditional Spelling in First Graders' Writing: Effects on Learning to Spell and Read." *Research in the Teaching of English* 22: 281–309.

Clay, M. 1985. *The Early Detection of Reading Difficulties*, 3rd. ed. Portsmouth, NH: Heinemann.

Dana, C., and Rodriguez, M. 1992. "TOAST: A System to Study Vocabulary." *Reading Research and Instruction* 31(4): 78–84.

Duffy, G., and McIntyre, L. 1982. "A Naturalistic Study of Instructional Assistance in Primary-Grade Reading." *Elementary School Journal* 83: 15–23.

Durkin, D. 1984. "Is There a Match Between What Elementary Teachers Do and What Elementary Manuals Recommend?" *Reading Teacher* 37: 734–744.

Durkin, D. 1989. *New Kindergarten Basal Reader Materials: What's a Teacher Supposed to Do with All This?* (Tech. Rep. #475). Urbana-Champaign, IL: University of Illinois Center for the Study of Reading.

Jenkins, J., Stein, M., and Wysocki, K. 1984. "Learning Vocabulary Through Reading." *American Educational Research Journal* 21: 767–789.

Kletzien, S. 1991. "Strategy Use by Good and Poor Comprehenders Reading Expository Text of Differing Levels." *Reading Research Quarterly* 26: 67–86.

McKeown, M. G. 1985. "The Acquisition of Word Meaning from Context by Children of High and Low Ability." *Reading Research Quarterly* 15: 3–18.

Moore, D.W., and Moore, S. A. 1992. "Possible Sentences: An Update." In *Reading in the Content Areas: Improving Class-*

room *Instruction*, 3rd ed., E. K. Dishner, T. W. Bean, J. E. Readence, and D. W. Moore, eds., Dubuque, IA: Kendall/Hunt.

Perfetti, C. A., Beck, I., Bell, L. C., and Hughes, C. 1987. "Phonemic Knowledge and Learning to Read Are Reciprocal: A Longitudinal Study of First Grade Children." *Merrill-Palmer Quarterly* 33: 283–319.

Resnick, L. B., and Weaver, P. A. 1979. *Theory and Practice in Early Reading*. Hillsdale, NJ: Lawrence Erlbaum Assoc.

Searfoss, L., and Readence, J. E. 1994. *Helping Children Learn to Read*. Boston: Allyn and Bacon.

Stahl, S. A., and Kapinus, B. A., 1991. "Possible Sentences: Predicting Word Meanings to Teach Content Area Vocabulary." *Reading Teacher* 45: 36–43.

Walker, B. 1992. *Supporting Struggling Readers*. Portsmouth, NH: Heinemann.

## CHAPTER 8

### Each Child Is Unique

Bender, W. N. 1992. *Learning Disabilities*. Boston: Allyn and Bacon.

Bos, C. S., and Vaughn, S. 1988. *Strategies for Teaching Students with Learning and Behavioral Problems*. Boston: Allyn and Bacon.

Clay, M. 1979. *The Early Detection of Reading Difficulties*, 3rd. ed. Portsmouth, NH: Heinemann.

Colangelo, N., and David, G., eds. 1991. *Handbook of Gifted Education*. Boston: Allyn and Bacon.

Fleisher, L. S., Jenkins, J. R., and Pany, D. 1979. "Effects on Poor Readers' Comprehension of Training in Rapid Decoding." *Reading Research Quarterly* 25: 30–48.

Gambrell, L. B. 1990. "Introduction: A Themed Issue on Reading Instruction for At-Risk Students." *Journal of Reading* 33: 485–488.

Lipson, M. Y. 1991. *Assessment and Instruction of Reading Disability: An Interactive Approach*. New York: HarperCollins.

Masland, R. L., and Masland, M. W. 1988. *Prevention of Reading Failure*. Parkston, MD: York Press.

McCormick, S. 1987. *Remedial and Clinical Reading Instruction.* Columbus, OH: Merrill.

Orton, S. 1937. *Reading, Writing, and Speech Problems in Children.* New York: W. W. Norton.

Salzer, R. T. 1984. "Early Reading and Giftedness—Some Observations and Questions." *Gifted-Child Quarterly* 28: 95–96.

Shore, B., Cornell, D., Robinson, A., and Ward, V. 1991. *Recommended Practices in Gifted Education.* New York: Teachers College Press.

Walker, B. J. 1990. *Remedial Reading.* Washington, DC: National Education Association.

Ysseldyke, J., and Algozzine, B. 1990. *Special Education.* Boston: Houghton Mifflin.

## CHAPTER 9

### Whole Language: Caution

Altwerger, B., Edelsky, C., and Flores, B. 1987. "Whole Language: What's New?" *Reading Teacher* 41: 144–154.

Baskill, J., and Whitman, P. 1988. *Evaluation: Whole Language, Whole Child.* Toronto: Scholastic.

Berger, J. 1993. "Fighting over Reading." *New York Times,* 17 Nov.: B1 and B6.

Brown, H., and Camboume, B. 1990. *Read and Retell: A Strategy for the Whole Language/Natural Learning Classroom.* Portsmouth, NH: Heinemann.

Chall, J. 1992. "The New Reading Debates: Evidence from Science, Art, and Ideology." *Reading Teacher* 94: 315–327.

Chaney, C. 1990. "Evaluating the Whole Language Approach to Language Arts: Pros and Cons." *Language, Speech, and Hearing Services in Schools* 21: 244–249.

Dechant, E. 1991. *Understanding and Teaching Reading.* Hillsdale, NJ: Lawrence Erlbaum Assoc.

Edelsky, C., Altwerger, B., and Flores, B. 1991. *Whole Language, What's the Difference?* Portsmouth, NH: Heinemann.

Fielding, L. G., Wilson, P. T., and Anderson, R. C. 1986. "A New Focus on Free Reading: The Role of Trade Books in Reading Instruction." In *Contexts of School-Based Literacy,* T. E. Raphael, ed. New York: Random House.

Flesch, R. 1983. *Why Johnny Still Can't Read*. New York: Harper.

Goodman, K. S. 1986. *What's Whole in Whole Language?* Portsmouth, NH: Heinemann.

Goodman, K. S., Smith, E. B., Meredith, R., and Goodman, Y. M. 1987. *Language and Thinking in School: A Whole Language Curriculum*, 3rd ed. New York: Richard Owen.

Goodman, Y. 1989. "Roots of the Whole Language Movement." *Elementary School Journal* 90: 113–128.

Kasten, W. C., and Clarke, B. K. 1989. *Reading/Writing Readiness for Preschool and Kindergarten Children: A Whole Language Report*. Florida Educational Research Council Research Project Report. Sarasota, FL: University of South Florida.

Liberman, I. Y., and Liberman, A. M. 1990. "Whole Language Versus Code-Emphasis: Underlying Assumptions and Their Implications for Reading Instruction." *Annals of Dyslexia* 40: 51–76.

Newman, J. 1985. *Whole Language: Theory in Use*. Portsmouth, NH: Heinemann.

Norris, J., and Damico, J. 1990. "Whole Language in Theory and Practice: Implications for Language Intervention." *Language, Speech, and Hearing Services in Schools* 21: 212–220.

Rhodes, L. K., and Shanklin, N. 1993. *Windows into Literacy*. Portsmouth, NH: Heinemann.

Stanovich, K. E., 1994. "Romance and Reality." *Reading Teacher* 47: 4.

Stauffer, R. G. 1980. *The Language Experience Approach to the Teaching of Reading*. New York: Harper and Row.

Tangel, D. M., and Blanchman, B. A. 1992. "Effect of Phoneme Awareness Instruction on Kindergarten Children's Invented Spelling." *Journal of Reading Behavior* 24: 233–261.

Teale, W. H., and Sulzby, E. 1986. *Emergent Literacy: Writing and Reading*. Norwood, NJ: Ablex.

Truch, S. 1991. *The Missing Parts of Whole Language*. Calgary: Foothills Educational Materials.

Vellutino, F. 1991. "Introduction to Three Studies on Reading Acquisition: Convergent Findings on Theoretical Foundations of Code-Oriented Versus Whole Language Approaches to Reading Instruction." *Journal of Educational Psychology* 83: 407–410.

Watson, D. 1989. "Defining and Describing Whole Language." *Elementary School Journal* 90: 129–141.

Weaver, C. 1994. *Reading Process and Practice, From Socio-Psychol- inguistics to Whole Language,* 2nd ed. Portsmouth, NH: Heinemann.

Yeager, D. 1991. *The Whole Language Companion.* Glenview, IL: Goodyear.

## CHAPTER 10

### Reading Recovery: Working at Success

Allington, R. 1992. "How to Get Information on Several Proven Programs for Accelerating the Progress of Low-Achieving Children." *Reading Teacher* 46: 246—248.

Clay, M. 1979. *The Early Detection of Reading Difficulties,* 3rd ed. Portsmouth, NH: Heinemann.

Clay, M. 1987. *Writing Begins at Home: Preparing Children for Writing Before They Go to School.* Portsmouth, NH: Heinemann.

Clay, M. 1991. *Becoming Literate: The Construction of Inner Control.* Portsmouth, NH: Heinemann.

Clay, M. 1993. *An Observation Survey of Early Literacy Achievement.* Portsmouth, NH: Heinemann.

Clay, M. 1993. *Reading Recovery: A Guidebook for Teachers in Training.* Portsmouth, NH: Heinemann.

DeFord, D. E., Lyons, C. A., and Pinnell, G. S. 1991. *Bridges to Literacy.* Portsmouth, NH: Heinemann.

Geeke, P. 1988. *Evaluation Report on the Reading Recovery Field Trial in Central Victoria, 1984.* Wollongong, Australia: Centre for Studies in Literacy, University of Wollongong.

Hamill, J. 1991. "As We See it: Classroom Teachers View Reading Recovery." *Reading Horizons* (June) 31: 439–448.

Jones, N. K. 1991. "Helping to Learn: Components and Principles of Reading Recovery Training." *Reading Horizons* (June) 31: 421–438.

Pinnell, G. S. 1990. "Success for Low Achievers through Reading Recovery." *Educational Leadership* (Sept.) 48: 17–21.

Pinnell, G. S., DeFord, D. E., and Lyons, C. A. 1988. *Reading Recovery: Early Intervention for At-Risk First Graders.* Arlington, VA: Educational Research Service.

Pinnell, G. S., Fried, M. D., and Estice, R. M. 1990. "Reading Recovery: Learning How to Make a Difference." *Reading Teacher* 43: 282–295.

Pinnell, G. S., Lyons, C. A., DeFord, D. E., Bryk, A. S., and Seltzer, M. 1994. "Comparing Instructional Models for the Literacy Education of High-Risk First Graders." *Reading Research Quarterly* 29(1): 9–39.

Stewart, P. A. 1990. "Reading Recovery: An Early Intervention Program." *Ohio Reading Teacher* (Fall) 25: 30–36.

Wasik, B. A., and Slavin, R. E. 1993. "Preventing Early Reading Failure with One on One Tutoring: A Review of Five Programs." *Reading Research Quarterly* (April-June) 28: 178–200.

Wheeler, H. G. 1986. "Reading Recovery: Central Victorian Field Trials." Unpublished manuscript. Bendigo, Australia: Bendigo College of Education.

## CHAPTER 11

### Writing

Barnhart, J. E. 1991. "An Analysis of Writing and Young Children's Literacy Acquisition." *Literacy Research Report* No. 6. DeKalb, IL: Northern Illinois University.

Brown, J., Phillips, L., and Stephens, E. 1992. *Toward Literacy: Theory and Applications for Teaching Writing in the Content Areas.* Belmont, CA: Wadsworth.

Bryant, P. E., and Bradley, L. 1983. "Why Children Sometimes Write Words They Do Not Read." In *Cognitive Processes in Spelling*, U. Frith, ed. London: Academic Press.

Buchanan, E. 1989. *Spelling in Whole Language Classrooms.* Katonah, NY: Richard C. Owen.

Calkins, L. M. 1986. *The Art of Teaching Writing.* Portsmouth, NH: Heinemann.

Clay, M. 1987. *Writing Begins at Home: Preparing Children for Writing Before They Go to School.* Portsmouth, NH: Heinemann.

Cooper, J. D. 1993. *Literacy: Helping Children Construct Meaning.* Boston: Houghton Mifflin.

Ehri, L. C. 1987. "Learning to Read and Spell Words." *Journal of Reading Behavior* 19: 5–31.

Fearn, L. 1983. *Developmental Writing in Elementary and Middle School*. San Diego, CA: Kabyn Books.

Flower, L. S., and Hayes, J. R. 1981. "Problem-Solving and the Cognitive Process of Writing." In *Writing: The Nature, Development, and Teaching of Written Communication*, C. H. Frederiksen and J. F. Dominic, eds. Hillsdale, NJ: Erlbaum.

Gentry, J. 1987. *Spell . . . Is a Four Letter Word*. Portsmouth, NH: Heinemann.

Gentry, J., and Gillet, J. W. 1993. *Teaching Kids to Spell*. Portsmouth, NH: Heinemann.

Graves, D. H. 1983. *Writing: Teachers and Children at Work*. Portsmouth, NH: Heinemann.

Graves, D., and Stuart, V. 1985. *Write from the Start*. New York: New American Library.

Hansen, J. 1987. *When Writers Read*. Portsmouth, NH: Heinemann.

Jongsma, K. 1990. "Reading-Spelling Links." *Reading Teacher* 43: 608–610.

Juel, C., and Roper-Schneider, D. 1985. "The Influence of Basal Readers on First Grade Reading." *Reading Research Quarterly* 20: 134–152.

Langer, J. A. 1986. *Children Reading and Writing: Structures and Strategies*. Norwood, NJ: Ablex.

Langer, J. A., and Applebee, A. N. 1987. *How Writing Shapes Thinking: A Study of Teaching and Learning*. Urbana, IL: National Council of Teachers of English.

McGinley, W., Pearson, P. D., Spiro, R. J., Copeland, K., and Tieney, R. J. 1989. *The Effects of Reading and Writing upon Thinking and Learning* (Tech. Rep. No. 477). Urbana-Champaign: University of Illinois, Center for the Study of Reading.

Moffett, J., and Wagner, B. J. 1983. *Student-Centered Language Arts and Reading, K-13: A Handbook for Teachers*. Boston: Houghton Mifflin.

Moore, D. W., and Moore, S. A. 1992. "Possible Sentences: An Update." In *Reading in the Content Area: Improving Classroom Instruction*, 3rd ed., E. K. Dishner, T. W. Bean, J. E. Readence, and D. W. Moore, eds. Dubuque, IA: Kendall/Hunt.

Newman, J. 1985. *The Craft of Children's Writing*. Portsmouth, NH: Heinemann.

Preece, A., and Cowden, D. 1993. *Writers in the Making: Sharing Processes with Parents*. Portsmouth, NH: Heinemann.

Readence, J. E., Bean, T. W., and Baldwin, R. S. 1995. *Content Area Reading: An Integrated Approach*, 5th ed. Dubuque, IA: Kendall/Hunt.

Rubin, A., and Hansen, J. 1986. "Reading and Writing: How Are the First Two R's Related?" In *Reading Comprehension: From Research to Practice*, J. Orasanu, ed. Hillsdale, NJ: Erlbaum.

Stahl, S. A., and Kapinus, B. A. 1991. "Possible Sentences: Predicting Word Meanings to Teach Content Area Vocabulary." *Reading Teacher* 45: 36–43.

Temple, C., Nathan, R. G., and Burns, N. A. 1988. *The Beginnings of Writing*, 2nd ed. Boston: Allyn and Bacon.

Wrobleski, L., 1990. "A Tip from a Teacher: The Writer's Briefcase." *Young Children* 45: 69.

## CHAPTER 12

### The School Program

Anderson, I. W., ed. 1984. *Learning to Read in American Schools*. Hillsdale, NJ: Erlbaum.

Bohan, H., and Bass, J. 1991. "Teaching Thinking in Elementary Mathematics and Science." *Educator's Forum* Fall: 1–10.

Brooks, S. E., Goodman, K. S., and Meredith, R. 1970. *Language and Thinking in School*. New York: Holt, Rinehart, and Winston.

Bush, C., and Heubner, M. 1979. *Strategies for Reading in the Elementary School*. New York: Macmillan.

Chall, J., 1983. *Learning to Read: The Great Debate*, rev. ed. New York: McGraw Hill.

Choate, T. J. 1987. *Assessing and Programming Basic Curriculum Skills*. Boston: Allyn and Bacon.

Cioffi, G. 1992. "Perspective and Experience: Developing Critical Reading Abilities." *Journal of Reading* 36: 48–52.

Devine, T. 1989. *Teaching Reading in the Elementary School: From Theory to Practice*. Boston: Allyn and Bacon.

Duffy, G. G., and Roehler, L. R. 1987. "Teaching Reading Skills as Strategies." *Reading Teacher* 40: 411–418.

Durkin, D. 1978–1979. "What Classroom Observations Reveal About Reading Comprehension." *Reading Research Quarterly* 14: 481–533.

Farr, R., and Carey, R. F. 1986. *Reading: What Can Be Measured?* Newark, DE: International Reading Association.

Fries, C., Fries, A. C., Wilson, R. G., and Rudolph, M. K., eds. 1966. *Merrill Linguistic Readers*. Columbus, OH: Charles E. Merrill Books.

Gates, A. I. 1928. *New Methods in Primary Reading*. New York: Columbia University Press.

Goodman, K. S. 1986. *What's Whole in Whole Language?* Portsmouth, NH: Heinemann.

Goodman, K. S., Shannon, P., Freeman, Y. S., and Murphy, S. 1988. *Report Card on Basal Readers*. Katonah, NY: Richard C. Owen.

Johnson, P. 1985. "Teaching Students to Apply Strategies that Improve Reading Comprehension." *Elementary School Journal* 85: 635–644.

Karlin, R. 1973. *Perspectives on Reading*. New York: Harcourt Brace Jovanovich.

Lyman, H. B. 1991. *Test Scores and What They Mean*. Englewood Cliffs, NJ: Prentice-Hall.

Matthews, M. M. 1966. *Teaching to Read: Historically Considered*. Chicago: University of Chicago Press.

McCracken, G., and Walcutt, C. C. 1963. *Lippincott's Basic Reading*. Philadelphia: J. B. Lippincott.

National Commission on Excellence in Education. 1983. *A Nation at Risk: The Imperatives of Educational Reform*. Washington, DC: U.S. Department of Education.

Osborne, J., Wilson, P. T., and Anderson, R. C., eds. 1985. *Reading Education: Foundations for a Literate America*. Lexington, MA: Lexington Books.

Pearson, P. D., and Dole, J. A. 1988. "Explicit Comprehension Instruction: A Review of Research and a New Conceptualization of Instruction." *Elementary School Journal* 88: 151–165.

Richardson, J., and Morgan, P. F. 1994. *Reading to Learn in the Content Areas*. Belmont, CA: Wadsworth.

Sochor, E. E. 1959. "The Nature of Critical Reading." *Elementary English* 36: 47–58.

Van Tassel-Baska, J. 1992. *Effective Curriculum Planning for Gifted Learners.* Denver: Love Publishing.


## CHAPTER 13

### What Parents Can Do

Adams, A., and Harrison, C. 1975. "Using Television to Teach Specific Reading Skills." *Reading Teacher* 29(1): 45–51.

Anderson, J. 1993. "Relationships Between Parents' Perceptions of Literacy Acquisition and Their Children's Early Literacy Acquisition." Paper presented at the annual meeting of the Canadian Society for the Study of Education.

Anderson, R. C., Wilson, P. T., and Fielding, L. G. 1988. "Growth in Reading and How Children Spend Their Time Outside of School." *Reading Research Quarterly* 23: 285–303.

Beentjes, J. W., and Van der Voort, T. H. 1988. "Television's Impact on Children's Reading Skills: A Review of Research." *Reading Research Quarterly* 23(4): 389–413.

Bergstrom, J. 1988. "Help Your Child Find Great Alternatives to Television." *PTA Today* 13(6): 15–17.

Binkley, M. R., ed. 1988. *Becoming a Nation of Readers: What Parents Can Do.* Washington, DC: Office of Educational Research and Improvement, U.S. Department of Education.

Bosworth, P. 1986. "A Case for Reading Aloud to Your Kids." *Working Woman* 11: 119.

Choat, E., and Griffin, H. 1986a. "Young Children, Television, and Learning, Part 1: The Effects on Children Watching a Continuous Off Air Broadcast." *Journal of Educational Television* 12(2).

Choat, E., and Griffin, H. 1986b. "Young Children, Television, and Learning, Part 2. Comparison of the Effects of Reading and Story Telling by the Teacher and Television Story Viewing." *Journal of Educational Television* 12(2).

Clay, M. 1987. *Writing Begins at Home: Preparing Children for Writing Before They Go to School.* Portsmouth, NH: Heinemann.

Fitzpatrick, K. 1992. "Attention Parents! Your Preschool Child and Reading." *Reading Improvement* 19: 50–53.

Greenfield, P. 1984. *Mind and Media—The Effects of Television, Video Games, and Computers.* Cambridge, MA: Harvard University Press.

Handel, R. 1991. *The Partnership for Family Reading: A Collaboration of Montclair State College and Newark Public Schools.* Upper Montclair, NJ: Montclair State College.

Hiebert, E. H., ed. 1991. *Literacy for a Diverse Society: Perspectives, Programs, and Policies.* New York: Teachers College Press.

Hinds, S. 1985. "The Joy of Reading." *Parents' Magazine* 60: 100–102.

Huck, C. 1992. "Developing Lifetime Readers." *Journal of Youth Services in Libraries* 5(4): 371–382.

Mcfarlane, E. C. 1994. *Children's Literacy Development: Suggestions for Parental Involvement.* ERIC Clearinghouse on Reading, English, and Communication, Bloomington, IN. Washington, DC: Office of Educational Research and Improvement.

McKay, D. 1981. "Introducing Preschool Children to Reading through Parent Involvement." Paper presented at the annual meeting of the Parents and Reading Conference on January 30, 1981, in New York.

Moody, K. 1980. *Growing Up on Television—The TV Effect.* New York: Times Books.

Morgan, M. 1980. "Television Viewing and Reading: Does More Equal Better?" *Journal of Communication* 30(1): 159–165.

Morrow, L. 1985. *Promoting Voluntary Reading in School and Home: Fastback No. 225.* Bloomington, IN: Phi Delta Kappa.

Neuman, S. 1980. "Television: Its Effects on Reading and School Achievement." *Reading Teacher* 34: 801–805.

Neuman, S. 1988. "The Displacement Effect: Assessing the Relation Between Television Viewing and Reading Performance." *Reading Research Quarterly* 23(4): 414–440.

Neuman, S. 1991. *Literacy in the Television Age: The Myth of the TV Effect.* Norwood, NJ: Ablex.

Postman, N. 1985. *Amusing Ourselves to Death: Public Discourse in the Age of Television.* New York: Penguin Books.

Preece, A., and Cowden, D. 1993. *Writers in the Making: Sharing Processes with Parents.* Portsmouth, NH: Heinemann.

*Read to Me: Recommended Literature for Children Ages Two Through Seven*. Sacramento, CA: California State Department of Education.

Reinking, D., and Wu, J. 1990. "Reexamining the Research on Television and Reading." *Reading Research and Instruction* 29(2): 30–43.

Roberts, D. 1984. "Reading and Television: Predictors of Reading Achievement at Different Age Levels." *Communication Research* 11(1): 9–49.

Schulman, M. 1993. "How to Inspire a Love of Reading." *Parents' Magazine* 68: 104–106.

Simic, M., and Smith, C. 1990. "Involving Parents in the Reading Process." *Learning Package No. 7*. Bloomington, IN: Indiana University School of Education.

Spiegel, D., and Lee, D. 1993. "Parental Perceptions of Literacy Development: Implications for Home-School Partnerships" *Young Children* 48: 74–79.

Teale, W. H. 1986. "Home Background and Young Children's Literacy Development." In *Emergent Literacy: Writing and Reading*, W. H. Teale and E. Sulzby, eds. Norwood, NJ: Ablex.

Tizard, J., Schofield, N. W., and Hewison, J. 1982. "Collaborations Between Teachers and Parents in Assisting Children's Reading." *British Journal of Educational Psychology* 52: 1–15.

Torrey, J. W. 1969. "Learning to Read Without a Teacher: A Case Study." *Elementary English* 46: 550–556.

Trelease, J. 1982. *The New Read-Aloud Handbook*. New York: Penguin Books.

Trelease, J. 1986. "Why Reading Aloud Makes Learning Fun." *U.S. News and World Report* 100: 65–66.

"TV or Not TV: That is the Question." 1993. *Reading Today* 11(2): 31.

Vukelich, C. 1984. "Parent's Role in the Reading Process: A Review of Practical Suggestions and Ways to Communicate with Parents." *Reading Teacher* 37: 472–477.

Zoglin, R. 1990. "Is TV Ruining Our Children?" *Time* 15 Oct.: 75–76.

Zuckerman, D. 1980. "Television Viewing, Children's Reading, and Related Classroom Behavior." *Journal of Communication* 30(1): 166–174.

# Index

**About the Author**

SEYMOUR W. ITZKOFF has been involved with education and the schools for almost 40 years—as a teacher in public schools, curriculum coordinator, Director of the Smith College Campus School, and Professor of Education at Hunter College and at Smith College since 1965. He is the author of 13 books on educational theory, reading, music, philosophy, evolutionary theory, and the science of intelligence.